Social Work with Children

Marian Brandon

Gillian Schofield

Liz Trinder

with Nigel Stone

MACMILLAN

First published 1998 by
MACMILLAN PRESS LTD
Houndmills, Basingstoke, Hampshire RG21 6XS
and London
Companies and representatives throughout the world

ISBN 0–333–65857–4

A catalogue record for this book is available
from the British Library.

This book is printed on paper suitable for recycling and made
from fully managed and sustained forest sources.

10 9 8 7 6 5 4 3 2 1
07 06 05 04 03 02 01 00 99 98

Editing and origination by
Aardvark Editorial, Suffolk

Printed in Malaysia

Contents

Acknowledgements

Our thanks go to friends and colleagues in the School of Social Work for all their encouragement. We owe a debt to the many different child care practitioners who have worked with us at the University of East Anglia and shared their knowledge and experience of working with children. Most importantly, we thank all the children who have talked to us and taught us about how they feel about their world.

Introduction

The case for social work with children

Work with children can be the most challenging but also the most rewarding part of the child and family social worker's role. It includes the face-to-face work when social workers are alongside children, listening to them express their ideas and feelings, finding ways of communicating with them that are appropriate and respectful, and fully involving them when decisions need to be made that affect them. It draws on the capacity to listen without being overwhelmed and to offer a relationship to a child who may be both vulnerable yet hostile or suspicious. It may involve observing a baby about whom there are concerns, using play materials with a disabled pre-school child, doing life-story work with a child in foster care or counselling a pregnant teenager. Such work can undoubtedly be extremely demanding of the social worker's personal and professional resources. It requires knowledge, skills and an agency context that can support it. Although there are many ways in which the social worker appropriately works *for* or *on behalf of* the child, these will not be the main focus of this book. We plan, instead, to focus on the wide-ranging potential for work with the child. Our starting point must be the principle that, as Lady Justice Elizabeth Butler-Sloss put it, children must be treated as 'persons' and not as 'objects of concern' (HMSO, 1988).

This professional commitment to working directly with children has been reinforced by the terms of both the United Nations Convention on the Rights of the Child (the UN Convention) and the Children Act 1989. Children not only have the right to have their welfare protected but also have the right to be consulted and to have their wishes and feelings taken into account. Neither the right to welfare nor the right to a voice can be achieved by children without the commitment of adults. For the child in need or in need of protection who is referred to a social services department, it is the social worker who must take responsibility

1

for ensuring both that the child's welfare is protected and that the child's voice is heard. We would argue that these two are inseparable. However, many important tasks are competing for that finite resource – the social worker's time – and social work with children is too easily overlooked or given low priority. It is therefore necessary to give careful consideration to ways of defining and defending the principles and practice of working with children.

If we begin at the beginning, it is worth setting out some of the key arguments for working with children:

- Children have rights and needs, just like adults, to have their views and feelings heard and to be treated with respect. They need to be able to talk to adults they trust.
- Children themselves are saying that they want the opportunity to have their voices heard.
- If children are able to communicate with social workers, social workers will become more knowledgeable about each child's experience of and perspective on her world. This is an essential starting point for any assessment or intervention in a child's life.
- Children who have experienced separation and loss, abuse or neglect, or have not grown up in their own families, may need extra help from social workers to understand what has happened to them. Most of these children will also need emotional support to come to terms with such experiences.
- Children who are in serious trouble in areas of their lives, for example being involved in delinquency or drug misuse, need to know that someone is prepared to see them as worth talking with and listening to.
- Children need to develop self-esteem and a sense of self-efficacy. They need to know that their views are taken into account when decisions are made.
- In a complex world, some children will need skilled and committed adults to advocate on their behalf.

Not all of this work can or should be undertaken by social workers in all cases. Some children will turn to foster carers; others may need to be offered the specialised help of other professionals, such as psychotherapists or psychologists. However, all children will need social workers who are able to communicate effectively with them and build a relationship with them. Without these basic skills, social workers will not be able to meet their responsibilities to the child.

Work with the child may seem an obvious priority for child care social workers, yet it remains a rather difficult and controversial area to define. In particular, there are concerns that talking with them about their feelings or using play techniques with children is in some way too specialised and therapeutic for social workers, who are busy enough with the difficult matter of dealing with the everyday world of the child, the school, the housing problems, the contact arrangements. In response to such dilemmas, Clare Winnicott offered this definition of the distinctive and special role of social work with children:

> The social worker starts off as a real person concerned with the external events and people in the child's life. In the course of her work with the child she will attempt to bridge the gap between the external world and his feelings about it and in doing so she will enter his inner world too. As a person who can move from one world to another, the social worker can have a special value all her own for the child and a special kind of relationship. (Winnicott 1964:45)

The social worker is able to operate effectively within the outer world of the child, to talk to parents and teachers, to be concerned about poor housing, to visit the hospital or the children's home, to attend if required at the police station. The social worker needs to understand and be effective within such systems. However, at the same time, the social worker needs to be thinking about and with the child, to attempt to see this world through the child's eyes and to discover not just how the outer world is affecting the child in an objective sense but how it is being experienced subjectively. It is this process which needs a whole range of additional skills. It requires the social worker to engage with the child, in ways appropriate to the age, understanding and circumstances of the child. It needs the social worker to have a proper understanding of how children develop and see the world, what children need from their environment and how they react if those needs are not met.

What the social worker learns from these two different worlds, the inner and the outer, helps her to make connections and enables her to work with the child to make sense of his experience and begin to answer some of the most troubling questions. What has the child found most upsetting about his parent's divorce? What could be the reasons for this child's stealing or that child's rejection by his parents? Once these connections are made, the worker and the child can then find a way forward in defining what is most helpful in both worlds.

What does the child need to do emotionally to come to terms with the divorce and grieve for the loss, but also what practical arrangements for contact would facilitate this process? How can the emotional basis of the child's stealing or the feelings of peer pressure be resolved with the child, but also how can a well-argued probation report for the court or a well-presented opinion at a case conference avoid a serious escalation of the practical consequences of the stealing? At all times, work with the child, however intensive it may be, happens in the context of the child's total environment – the family, the playgroup, the school, the street corner. It also happens within the procedural boundaries of the social work agency and the professional boundaries of the social work role.

From the children's point of view, the fact that the social worker knows about and understands their world and works within it is very important both practically and symbolically. The child in foster care may be worried about how his mother is faring in the psychiatric hospital. The practical arrangements for contact will matter, and so also will the fact that the social worker knows his mother and has visited her in hospital. The child needs in some way to make links. The social worker can help the child to make connections between past and present and understand the whys and wherefores, can listen to the child's ideas and feelings, but is also herself a connection between different worlds.

Throughout this process, the child is a full participant. It is the social worker's task to maximise the child's capacity to express his wishes and feelings, not just about the major decisions as defined in the Children Act 1989 but in all areas of the work that affect the child. Where to see the child, what materials to use, how frequently and with what purpose – these all need to be carefully discussed with the child, as they will have been with parents or carers. Talking with the child, listening to the child and taking the child's feelings into account alongside all the other sources of information and opinion in a case is a complex process that needs commitment from the worker if it is to be sensitively handled and effective.

Outline of contents

This book will provide some theoretical and practical guidance so that social workers have a clear sense of:

● what they need to know before they work with children

- what they need to know before they work with this particular child in these particular circumstances
- what the worker and child can do together
- how to be a better practitioner with children.

In planning this book, we have set out to provide a historical, legal, and developmental framework for social work with children and have then selected major areas of social work activity in which to apply theory and principles to practice. Part One begins by offering a historical overview of the relationship between children, families and the state. An analysis of the nature of child welfare services traces the movement from child rescue to children's rights and comments on the history of child care social work practice in working with children. The second half of Chapter 1 looks in more detail at the rights of children in the legislative context of the Children Act 1989. Chapter 2 then provides an account of development in childhood, making connections between emotional, social and behavioural development and highlighting those areas which the social worker needs to be aware of when working with children.

Part Two begins in Chapter 3 with a look at the basic principles, skills and techniques for work with children, which can be adapted to a wide range of social work situations. The need to plan the work, the importance of thinking about the child's context and the use of direct and indirect techniques for engaging the child are all covered. Examples will be given of work with children of different ages.

In Chapter 4, we explore the social work role with children in need and children in need of protection. Very little has been written about the social work task in listening to children, particularly younger children, who are at home with their families. Although it has often been suggested in enquiry reports that children at home need to be listened to (Stone 1991; Bridge Child Care Consultancy 1995), very little attention has been paid to the kind of work that is possible or, very importantly, to what processes of negotiation with birth families may be necessary to enable this work to happen. Inevitably, the work with the child is part of a complex network of social work activity involving the birth family and the professional networks.

Chapter 5 covers another difficult area of practice–work with the child during care and adoption proceedings in the courts. The need to offer children support and someone to talk to and trust when their future is to be decided in court may appear obvious. What is less obvious is how the social worker who takes the case to court can also be that trusted person and what the basic principles for this area of work are. The role of the guardian ad litem is relevant here and, as a specialised branch of social work, it will be described. Working relationships between the social worker and the guardian, and their ability to co-operate and negotiate relationships with the child, will also be explored.

For children who are separated from their families and are looked after by the local authority in foster or residential care, the need for the child to make sense of his loss and participate in plans for the future will have significant implications for the focus of work. Chapter 6 explores the range of methods and skills that are relevant for working with children who are looked after. In a climate of concern about the quality of services to children in care or accommodation, it is important for social workers to be clear about what is a model of good practice in relation to their work with the child.

Although the Children Act demands that courts treat the child's welfare as paramount, this principle does not apply in the criminal justice system. Society's fear of and anger towards young offenders makes it difficult for social workers and probation officers to hold the line, to encourage courts to continue to see children as children. Chapter 7 analyses the legal and research framework and explores the issues in a way that will assist practitioners involved in working with young offenders.

Finally, the conclusion uses the themes identified in the book to identify what changes will be necessary if social work as a profession is to redefine and further develop its work with children.

PART ONE

The Context of Social Work with Children

1

Child Care Policy, Children's Rights and The Children Act

Introduction

Beginning in the nineteenth and accelerating in the twentieth century, children's rights to protection have been increasingly defined, articulated and enforced. Over the past 20 years, this protective stance has been supplemented with the promotion of the rights of children to participate in decisions affecting their lives. In the now famous phrase of Lady Justice Butler-Sloss, there has been a move towards treating the child as 'a person and not an object of concern'.

Our aim in this chapter is to locate current social work practice with children within a historical and legal context. The chapter is in two parts. In the first half, we trace the development of policy and practice towards children and children's rights over the past two centuries, examining social work with children in the context of wider social policy trends. In the second half of the chapter, we look in greater detail at contemporary understandings of children's rights underpinning social work with children. Our discussion here will focus on the broad groups of rights – protection, participation, anti-discrimination and development – set out in the UN Convention and especially the Children Act 1989.

Some people may wonder why we are pausing to look at historical trends in social work with children. Why not just get straight down to the real business of work with children? Our answer is that we want people to think critically about what social work with children is for and what social work with children means. Skill or even knowledge by itself is not enough and can easily be misplaced or misdirected. Critical thinking or reflection is vital, and one of the best ways to think critically about the present is to have some understanding of how we arrived here. It is usually easier really to understand something by comparing it with something else. In this case, we can appreciate the extent to which children's rights are being taken seriously today by comparing this with

9

previous practice. It is also vital that we understand the wider forces that shape the development of social work. Like other disciplines – education or medicine – social work has been shaped forcefully by wider social, political, economic and intellectual trends. It has never existed in a vacuum. As we will see in this chapter, we can only make sense of particular social work practices, the emergence of children's rights being a good example, by looking at wider social trends. Finally, a historical understanding also alerts us to the danger of complacency. It soon becomes clear that every generation assumes that contemporary arrangements and practice are better than anything that has gone before and are the natural way of doing things. Like previous generations, there is a danger of complacency and a belief that we have got things right. An awareness of historical trends and how they inform current practices can be an essential antidote to complacency!

Types of child and types of right

It is important to begin by recognising that childhood itself is not a fact of life. Where and when we live fundamentally shapes how we think about and treat children, childhood and children's rights. As we will see, what it means to be a child, and what childhood is meant to be, is socially constructed, and each society constructs these meanings differently. Although the basic biological facts of life change little over time, there is nothing fixed in the way in which society handles these biological differences. As James and Prout (1990:7) put it:

> The immaturity of children is a biological fact of life but the ways in which this immaturity is understood and made meaningful is a fact of culture.

The white Western Disneyland version of a safe and dependent childhood differs starkly from global or historical realities. Every society, for example, has different ideas and rules about how long childhood lasts. Equally, societies differ in the degree to which they involve children in decisions that are made about them; indeed, some societies never even contemplate child involvement.

We can see, then, that different understandings or constructions of childhood produce different expectations and interpretations of children's behaviour. Historians of childhood have, in the past, argued fiercely over the meaning of childhood. The French historian Philippe Aries initiated the debate in the 1960s by claiming that a separate state of childhood did not really exist before the seventeenth century, children being treated as little adults. Since then, Aries' thesis has been subject to sustained critique (see Cunningham 1995 for a summary). In practice, it is more likely that there were a range of childhoods, with considerable variations in what it meant to be a child between class and region. Contradictory attitudes towards children remain commonplace, children being alternately constructed as innocent little angels and little devils innately capable of the worst types of crime until adequately socialised by adults.

The changing, and at times contradictory, meanings of childhood evident in the historical and sociological literature are mirrored in the development of child care policy, which has both reflected and created different versions of childhood. Our understanding of children's rights is strongly related to wider political and intellectual trends. For example, one of the most important political and intellectual themes of our times is empowerment, and this has strongly influenced contemporary interpretations of children's rights as participation rights.

In the following section, we will be looking at the way in which these two factors – the socio-political context and different ideas about children and childhood – have produced different understandings of children's rights in law and practice.

Early days: *laissez-faire* and child rescue

During the course of the nineteenth century, a more uniform and universalised notion of childhood gained ground. Until that time, the dominant experience for the majority of children had been contributing to the family income in paid or unpaid employment. In contrast, the 'ideal' childhood, which developed gradually during the nineteenth century, reinforced through state and voluntary initiatives, was based on the 'domestic ideal' of the early nineteenth century middle-class family (Hendrick 1990). This ideal was a childhood that saw children as qualitatively different from adults, whose special nature could be easily brutalised, debased and dangerous if they were allowed to become like adults and enter the adult world. As the nineteenth century developed, a range of protective measures were taken to render children dependent and to remove them from what was now to become the adult world of work into the child's world of the school and home.

Laws controlling child labour and the introduction of universal education in the nineteenth century recognised the need for children's protection and acknowledged that they had rights. Schooling weakened the link between childhood and labour. As school gradually took the place of work, and regular schooling became compulsory (around 1900 throughout Europe), the attitudes towards the place and role of children also changed. Childhood could last for longer and children could be seen as more dependent. For the first time, it became possible for parents not to see their children primarily as contributors to the family and an economic asset. It was now expected that goods would flow *from* parents to children rather than from children *to* parents.

For the emergent child welfare/social work organisations, the dominant concern was to 'save' children so that they could enjoy a childhood. All the voluntary societies, such as Dr Barnardos, were dedicated to rescuing children from bad environments, bad (adult) influences and bad parents, and providing them them with a fresh start where they could become children (Cleaver and Freeman 1995; Colton *et al.* 1995). The aim of child-saving was to resocialise children into the respectable working class from the morally lacking 'residuum'.

It is important, however, not to overstate the extent of social policy interventions. Although the nineteenth century witnessed a significant shift in ideas about children and childhood, the extent to which this was actively promoted was more limited. In terms of child care policy, the nineteenth century is best characterised by what Lorraine Fox Harding (1991) has called the 'Laissez-faire and patriarchy perspective', based on the preservation of family privacy and minimal state intervention in the family. From this perspective, there is a minimal place for welfare policy: all responsibility devolves to the family. Cleaver and Freeman (1995) argue that intervention was largely confined to situations outside the family. The role of the state in child care was governed by the the the Poor Law, which exemplified *laissez-faire* values of minimum intervention; this was to keep costs down and also to preserve the sanctity of family life. When intervention occurred, it was 'to rescue children from the absolutes of poverty and degradation' (Cleaver and Freeman 1995). It was not until 1889, when the National Society for the Prevention of Cruelty to Children was formed, that the family and the private details of family relationships could come under some scrutiny. However, the control of the family and the father in particular was hard to regulate and laws were 'grudgingly enacted' (Gordon 1989; Cleaver and Freeman 1995). Within the family, internal family decisions about childrearing and so on are the responsibility of the family's most powerful members, that is the parents, particularly the father. Indeed, it was not until 1886 that for the first time, the law in England placed the child's welfare *first*, before the conduct and wishes of the parents (Hoggett 1993). Thus, while the nineteenth century saw some moves towards articulating children's rights to protection, it was not until the following century that children's rights to participation were discussed.

By the end of the nineteenth century, life for the majority of children was very different from that of their predecessors. Medical, scientific and political developments had ensured that life for most of them would be more than a mere struggle for survival. In 1901 infant mortality was 161 deaths per 1,000 births and between 1928 and 1931 it had fallen to 66 deaths per 1,000 births (Hardyment 1983:159).

Development of state paternalism and child protection

During the late nineteenth and early twentieth century, there was a broad, if incomplete, shift in the West away from *laissez-faire* approaches to child welfare, with an accompanying reconceptualisation of childhood. In terms of child care policy, Fox Harding (1991) terms this 'State paternalism and child protection', predicated on extensive state intervention in the family to protect children from poor parental care (as defined by professionals). Building on the developments of the nineteenth century, childhood was seen as a distinct and vulnerable stage of the life cycle, requiring adult protection and adult decision-making. Both *laissez-faire* and paternalist perspectives shared a common view of children as having a limited capacity for self-determination and decision-making. The key difference during the twentieth century was the extent to which a different set of adults, that is social work and other professionals, increasingly supplemented parents as decision-makers for and protectors of children, as the state and its army of child care experts increasingly claimed a right to regulate the family. The rapid development of the social sciences and medicine provided a body of child welfare knowledge to underpin this. Sociologists, particularly those from the emerging discipline of child psychology, became increasingly important in defining the parameters of 'normal' family life and 'normal' childhood. Despite significant disagreements between them, the work of Burt, Isaacs, Klein, Winnicott and Bowlby was highly significant in highlighting for the first time the importance of the child's psychological life and the role of the family and parenting (Hendrick 1990).

As the twentieth century developed, the range of state services for children and families increased. Social work played a part in the comprehensive social policies of the new post-war welfare state to eradicate Beveridges's 'five giant evils' of want, disease, ignorance, squalor and idleness. With language that would appear in much later legislation, s.12 of the 1948 Children Act made it a duty of local authorities to further the child's best interests and 'afford him the opportunities for the proper development of his character and abilities'. Section 1 of the Act placed a duty on local authorities to 'make use of facilities and services available for children in the care of their own parents'. The newly formed Children's Departments' work changed from the legacy of the nineteenth century curative, rescue service to one with the virtually infinite brief of promoting the welfare of children by working with the family as a whole (Colton *et al.* 1995:7).The concept of 'prevention' developed in the 1950s and, furthered through casework, showed that most of Children's Departments were trying to prevent the admission of children into care (Packman 1993). The Children and Young Persons Act 1963 placed a duty on local authorities to help families whose children were not in the care of the local authority.

The 1970s were characterised by the organisational changes that have rolled on into the end of the century. The Seebohm Committee's recommendations of 1968 resulted in the creation of large comprehensive Social Services Departments and an expansion in the work to all client groups. The positive idealistic stance of the 'preventive' 1960s had been replaced by what Packman calls a gloomier analysis, leading to tougher interventions (Packman 1993:230).

Participation and procedure

The 1970s was probably the high watermark of state paternalism in child welfare. Since that time, social work, and the welfare state in general, has had to redefine itself in response to both internal and external critiques and challenges. The exponential growth in public expenditure was abruptly curtailed in the wake of the economic crises of the mid-1970s. From then on, child welfare has been framed within the context of economic scarcity.

Just as significant has been the intellectual and political challenge to state paternalism. The ascendancy of the welfare state and collectivism established after the Second World War has been swept back by an incoming tide of liberalism and individualism. The old group identifications of social class, work group, local community and family are breaking down, and individuals' reference points and identity have been rendered discontinuous and contingent (Jenks 1996:16). The focus has shifted away from collective needs and collective responses, and professional expertise and self-confidence, to the rights of individuals to define and defend their own interests. Increasingly, supposedly supportive interventions have been as bureaucratic and oppressive. The right argued increasingly for the freeing of individuals and families from the iron grip of the state. In a similar vein, critiques from radical and feminist social workers also questioned the controlling nature of much state intervention (Parton 1996). In terms of child care policies, Lyon and Parton (1995:46) identify a range of influential forces, including critiques of bureaucratic and oppressive state intervention, where the left and right have both found themselves arguing for far greater emphasis on individual rights as consumers or customers and much less emphasis on the state, community or even family to support us. Consumer choice, partnership and empowerment enable individuals, and less often communities or collectives, to be 'freed' to make their own decisions, at the same time as the services over which they are having more say are being eroded.

Against this backdrop of the breakdown of the post-war settlement and the increasing fragmentation of society, social work is attempting to reconcile two potentially contradictory trends, attempting both to manage (that is, to achieve more predictability, control of resources, scientific planning, prediction and assessment) and to empower and encourage partnership.

Social work with children over the past 20 years has been characterised by an increasing emphasis on tight procedural detail, with the investigation of injury or abuse becoming a key theme. For workers, there has been a strong sense of being under siege, criticisms coming not only from the press and media, but also from research, child death enquiries and governmental reviews. The public perception of social workers took a severe blow following the Colwell child death enquiry in the 1970s. Social workers were pilloried for allying themselves too closely to parents and 'the blood tie', as exemplified in the cases of Jasmine Beckford and, to an extent, Maria Colwell. Risk assessment and monitoring of possible maltreatment began to replace more supportive casework skills and 'helping' families with children living at home (Brandon 1996). Practice following the 1975 Children Act put an emphasis on the removal of children rather than on the social disadvantages that could be argued to have put them at risk in the first place (Colton *et al.* 1995:20). The report into the death of 4-year-old Jasmine Beckford, *A Child in Trust* (1985), warned of the dangers to the safety of the child if social workers became over-concerned with the problems of the parents. Jasmine was killed when living at home, on a Care Order, with her mother and stepfather. She died as a result of her stepfather's violence but had also been malnourished and abused over a long period of time (Reder *et al.* 1993:144). Such arguments constituted the beginning of implicit, if not explicit, criticism of 'supportive' social work. Child abuse was to be 'identified, predicted and prevented' (Parton 1991:58) in a diagnostic, scientific fashion.

At the same time, the direction of much of the work with children was set firmly away from preventive work with children in their own families towards securing 'psychological parents' elsewhere. This formed the backbone of the 'permanence movement', which was a response to the large numbers of children seen to be 'drifting' in care without plans (Rowe and Lambert 1973).

The shift towards more proceduralised and tougher practice did not, however, go unchallenged. The influential research publication *Social Work Decisions in Child Care* (1985) pointed to the fact that links with families for children in care were being overlooked and control was being confused with planning and that 'in a laudable desire to avoid drift and be "firmer", controls are imposed at a time and in a manner that is unconstructive and often counter productive' (HMSO 1985:19). The retreat into bureacracy and procedural detail was explained as a defence for workers who lacked support and who 'cannot tolerate the pain of getting involved and working with feelings' (1985:21).

The Cleveland Enquiry into professional assessment and intervention in cases of suspected child sexual abuse was unlike the child death inquiries in that it questioned over-zealous professional activity and came about as a result of parental complaints about allegations of sexual abuse. Protection should instead be offered to children from misguided intervention. While children needed protection:

> this must be achieved in a way that does not trample on the rights of parents and inflict unnecessary distress on the very children we wish to be helped. (Minister of State Tony Newton, in Parton 1991:114)

From the Cleveland Report onwards, policy and practice has increasingly emphasised the importance of working in partnership with parents. In treating the child 'as a person' rather than an 'object of concern', the child's subjective understanding of her own world needed to be first sought and then understood. Children's welfare could not be promoted solely by the application of scientific processes to assessment.

It is against this backdrop that we can make sense of the emergence of the two other child care perspectives identified by Fox Harding, both of which emphasise participation. Like the *laissez-faire* perspective, the 'parents' rights perspective' values the integrity of the family and opposes extensive state interference in family matters. Unlike the *laissez-faire* perspective, emphasis is placed on the potentially supportive role of the state in providing services to support parents in their role. The focus is on the family unit as a whole, rather than disaggregating it into its constituent parts. Reclaiming decision-making for parents from professionals is given greater weight than is respecting the autonomy of the child.

The fourth perspective, and the one which informs much of our contemporary discussion on children's rights, is labelled by Fox Harding as 'children's rights and children's liberation'. The focus shifts from children's need for protection either from or by parents, to children's rights to participation and autonomy. This perspective presents a contrasting construction of childhood. Children are seen as an oppressed group, (mistakenly) discriminated against on the basis of their age. Instead, writers within this perspective emphasise the rationality, competence and strength of children and minimise the differences between children and adults or the dependency and vulnerability of children. Children here become independent actors, with separate interests within the family. Children cannot and should not rely on their parents or professionals to act in their best interests, but must speak and act for themselves.

The pressure group activity apparent in the Cleveland Enquiry was occurring elsewhere through the 1970s and 80s. Pressure groups were becoming active on behalf of children and families involved in the child welfare system, making effective use of the new ideas about children's rights. The Voice of the Child in Care, the Children's Legal Centre and the National Association for Young People in Care (NAYPIC) all provided powerful new perspectives and criticisms from young people themselves about services and the experience of being in care (Packman 1993). The launch of ChildLine in 1986 also gave children living at home, not under the gaze of the welfare services, access to their own confidential helpline. The combination of these groups formed a powerful lobbying phalanx during the passage of what came to be the Children Act 1989.

At practice and policy level, the children's rights perspective was also increasingly evident during the 1980s. A range of developments resulted in children being taken seriously as people in their own right. The 'guardian ad litem' system provided a court-based independent worker on behalf of the child (see Chapter 5). Children were thus recognised as independent beings with their own interests who needed representation and also consultation. New areas of work emerged for some child care practitioners (often those in specialist fostering or adoption posts) in the 1980s, which had their theoretical origins in psychoanalytic traditions of the 1950s and 60s. Children placed with substitute parents would often undertake grief work, which could include 'life-story work'. Techniques of play therapy and relationship-building were disseminated through materials such as the BAAF teaching pack 'In Touch with Children' (1984) and through writers such as Fahlberg (1988) and Oaklander (1978). The aim of these materials was to encourage workers to take a much more active role in helping children to express their inner feelings (Aldgate and Simmonds 1988:14). While *Social Work Decisions in Child Care* had no particular place for the child's views in 1985, 3 years later the subsequent guide to child protection assessments from the Department of Health *Protecting Children: A Guide for Social Workers Undertaking a Comprehensive Assessment* (1988) had more explicit statements about the need to consult children and about their rights:

> Children and young persons who come to the notice of the helping professions because of difficulties they or their families are experiencing have a right to receive sensitive help and intervention. They have a right to be consulted and their views taken into account, having regard to their age and understanding, on matters and decisions which affect their lives. (Department of Health 1988:9)

In practice, however, most social workers spent little time with children. While a few workers before the 1989 Children Act were practising skills in working individually with children, most social workers rarely saw children on their own. *Social Work Decisions in Child Care* (HMSO 1985) commented that area team social workers appeared to lack the time and skills for direct work with children and that this work was left to others:

> There was little evidence to suggest that social workers were much involved in direct contact with children... The children's primary carers,

foster parents and residential staff were seen to have greater opportunities. Where skills beyond this were required, the social worker generally
referred the case to an acknowledged specialist in child development,
health or education. (National Children's Bureau, in HMSO 1985:14)

Most social workers saw children on their own 'at least sometime',
but this was often very brief 'and passed unnoticed by child and foster
parent' (Rowe, in HMSO 1985:14). Rowe acknowledged that these
rare occasions provided an opportunity for the child to speak
confidentially to the worker if she wished to do so but 'it was evidently
not something that the child could look forward to or count on'
(Rowe *et al.* 1984:159).

Thus, by the end of the 1980s, a range of issues and concerns had
come to influence child care policy and social work with children. A
range of ideas had developed about how best to protect children at the
same time as resources were under severe pressure and social workers
under intense public scrutiny. Towards the end of the decade, inititia-
tives on parent's rights and children's rights emerged, coexisting
somewhat uneasily with the emphasis on proceduralisation in social
work. The next section explores how some of these tensions in child
welfare – protection and participation, parents' and children's rights,
participation and proceduralisation – are addressed in the legal context
by the UN Convention and the Children Act 1989.

Writing children's rights

During the course of the 1970s and 80s, there were a range of significant developments on children's rights. At a theoretical level, writers
began seriously to develop and examine the concept of children's
rights; at governmental level, two highly significant children's rights
developments at the end of the 1980s were the UN Convention and
the Children Act 1989.

Liberators versus caretakers

Discussions of children's rights seem to have been enmeshed in a string
of binaries: between children as competent and incompetent, between
liberation and paternalism, between autonomy and welfare, between
liberators and caretakers. For the 'child liberators', the differences
between adults and children are seen to be less pronounced, the
implication being that children should be treated similarly to adults.

Self-determination is all. For the 'caretakers', children are seen as qualitatively different from adults. They are held to be less capable and more vulnerable than adults and hence require special protection and decisions being made on their behalf by adult caretakers (Archard 1993:55).

We will be arguing throughout this book that the rights versus welfare and similarity versus difference pairings are reductionist and do little to recognise the complexities of children as a group, the complexities of individual children or the complexities of their rights. King and Piper (1995) have raised concerns about the use of the concept of children's rights in the legal realm. They argue that rights language is reductionist:

> Children are at times reified and at other times treated as if they were little adults without child-like characteristics. The complexities and sensitivities of their emotional, physical and intellectual development do become simplified into legal precepts and rules of thumb which guide decision-making. (King and Piper 1995:144)

Researchers into childhood are becoming increasingly aware of the complexity of children's lives and the extent to which children define, as well as are defined by, their social worlds (see for example James and Prout 1996). Children differ by age, gender, ethnicity and disability. The ability of children to shape their world also differs depending on the situation in which they find themselves. Children's agency is different in the child-dominated and child-defined world of the playground from life in the classroom or family (James and Prout 1996). However, even in the family, careful research indicates how different parental expectations of children of the same age produces very different levels of autonomy in children (Solberg 1990). Discussions of whether children are autonomous or dependent, rational or irrational, seem therefore to miss the point. Children can be one, both or neither.

One possible way to avoid the dangers highlighted by King and Piper and to avoid a reductionist approach based on welfare versus autonomy is to take an expansive or inclusive view of children's rights, incorporating rights to both welfare and autonomy. We look in the next sections at attempts to produce such inclusive theories of children's rights, first by outlining the children's rights framework developed by Freeman and Eekelaar, and second by examining the broad stance on children's rights adopted by the UN Convention and the Children Act 1989.

Inclusive rights frameworks

Two of the best-known frameworks of children's rights are those of Michael Freeman (1983) and John Eekelaar (1986). While there are considerable overlaps between the two, we outline both of them here as they are particularly helpful in developing broadly based notions of rights.

Michael Freeman's theory of liberal paternalism

Freeman argues for the importance of thinking of children as rights-holders to whom certain entitlements are owed 'as of right' rather than out of compassion or benevolence. His theory of rights is founded on ensuring that children should participate in decision-making as much as they are capable, combined with a right to liberal paternalism, based on:

> what sorts of action or conduct would we wish, as children, to be shielded against on the assumption that we would want to mature to a rationally autonomous adulthood and be capable of deciding on our own system of ends as free and rational beings? We would choose principles that would enable children to mature to independent adulthood. (Freeman 1983:57)

On this basis, Freeman outlines four types of right:

- *Rights to welfare.* This is the broadest category of rights and refers to a broad set of claims to 'a happy childhood' as set out in the UN Declaration on the Rights of the Child (now superseded by the UN Convention). These include rights to education, nutrition and health and non-discrimination. Freeman argues that, while these rights are non-contentious, their global nature makes them difficult to both define and enforce.
- *Rights to protection.* In contrast with welfare rights, the second category is concerned with protecting children from harm, such as abuse, neglect and exploitation. Protective rights are rights that entitle children to a minimum standard of care. They are based on an assumption that children are a vulnerable grouping requiring protection, either from parents or, failing them, from the state.
- *The right to be treated like adults.* Freeman argues that the differential treatment of children and adults based on an arbitrary

age distinction is discriminatory. He argues that, on social justice grounds, children should be treated like adults. He does not follow the liberationist stance of writers of the 1970s who would abolish all distinctions between children and adults. Instead, he argues that age-related distinctions should be kept under constant review, decisions about the capacity of individual children being made on a case-by-case basis. As we will see, this is a similar approach to the Gillick competence formulation developed over the past decade.

● *Rights against parents.* The fourth type of right places parents in the role of representative for the child. Freeman argues that, in major decisions, parental decisions should hold sway but only if they are in accord with an 'objective' evaluation of whether they are in line with children's 'primary social goods', that is the things that any rational person would want to pursue. If not, an outside agency should supplant the representative role of the parent.

John Eekelaar's theory of children's rights

Like Freeman, John Eekelaar (1986) develops a framework of rights based on speculating 'what a child might retrospectively have wanted once it reaches a position of maturity' (1986:170). Eekelaar identifies three separate kinds of interest that form the basis of rights:

● *Basic interests* refer to a minimum standard of care (physical, emotional and intellectual). Parents/carers are required to avoid preventing or harming development. Where parents do not perform this task, for example in cases of abuse or neglect, the state may intervene.

● *Developmental interests* require parents and the state to ensure that all children should have an equal opportunity to maximise the resources available to them during their childhood.

● *Autonomy interest* refers to 'the freedom to choose his own lifestyle and to enter social relations according to his own inclinations uncontrolled by the authority of the adult world, whether parents or institutions'. Eekelaar argues that the autonomy interest, while being important, must be subordinate to basic and developmental interests on the basis that children, when they reach adulthood, will retrospectively argue for the primacy of basic or developmental interest over autonomy interests where there is a conflict.

The children's rights frameworks developed by Freeman and Eekelaar are interesting because they emphasise the range of rights that children may be thought to possess. Children here have rights to autonomy and participation as well as rights to development and protection. Both recognise that autonomy rights and other rights may clash, and both argue that, in such cases, adult determinations of what is best must trump children's wishes. As we will see, the UN Convention and the Children Act 1989 give children a range of 'welfare rights' and participation rights, the former ultimately holding sway.

The UN Convention

After 10 years of discussion and deliberation, the Convention was adopted by the UN General Assembly on 20 November 1989. To date, it has been ratified by more than 150 countries around the world, making it the most rapidly and widely ratified of all the UN conventions. The UN Convention was ratified by the UK government in December 1991. It contains more than 40 articles covering a very broad range of matters affecting children. These rights fall into four broad categories: rights to care or protection, participation and anti-discrimination and the right to the best possible development (Hammarberg 1995).

Rights to welfare/protection

Article 3 of the UN Convention sets out children's rights to welfare and protection. The article has two crucial components. The first emphasises that state and private institutions should have the 'best interests of the child' as a primary consideration throughout their work. The second component is that governments act to ensure that the child is adequately protected and cared for, taking into account the rights and duties of the child's carers. Article 19 requires that governments take all appropriate legislative, administrative, social and educational measures to protect children from abuse, neglect and exploitation from parents or carers. It also requires states to have effective procedures for prevention, identification, investigation and treatment in cases of child maltreatment.

Rights to best possible development

The provisions of the UN Convention go beyond attempts to secure protection from harm, Article 6.2 requiring states to promote the best possible development of the child:

> States Parties shall ensure to the maximum extent possible the survival and development of the child.

The Convention recognises that children are best cared for within their own families (Articles 5 and 18) but requires governments to offer 'appropriate assistance' to carers and to develop services for the care of children (Article 18.2). Given the gross inequalities in wealth that continue to exist between rich and poor countries, the expectation is not that all countries will be able to afford the same social policy provision for children; what Article 4 does require is that all governments undertake measures to promote children's economic, social and cultural rights to 'the maximum extent of their available resources'.

Participation rights

The UN Convention strongly promotes the right of children to participate in decision-making, although the weight given to the expressed views of the child will vary according to the age and maturity of the child. Article 12 states that:

> States Parties shall assure to the child who is capable of forming his or her own views the right to express those views freely in all matters affecting the child, the views of the child being given due weight in accordance with the age and maturity of the child.

The UN Convention sets out a range of other personal rights, all of which reinforce the status of the child as an independent human subject rather than just a passive object, and which are an essential component of participation rights. These include the right to an identity (a name and nationality from birth; Articles 7 and 8), rights of freedom of expression and information (Article 13), rights to freedom of conscience and association (Articles 14 and15), rights to privacy (Article 16) and rights to cultural expression (Article 30).

Rights to non-discrimination

The UN Convention makes two very important provisions on discrimination. First of all, it requires that the rights set out in the UN Convention apply equally to all children without discrimination of any kind (Article 2). To reinforce this, the UN Convention contains specific provisions for certain groups of children who face particular disadvantage:

> States Parties recognize that a mentally or physically disabled child should enjoy a full and decent life, in conditions which ensure dignity, promote self-reliance, and facilitate the child's active participation in the community. (Article 23.1)

and:

> In those States in which ethnic, religious or linguistic minorities or persons of indigenous origin exist, a child belonging to such a minority or who is indigenous shall not be denied the right, in community with other members of his or her group, to enjoy his or her own culture, to profess and practice his or her own religion, or to use his or her own language. (Article 30)

Having ratified the UN Convention, the UK government has bound itself to act in accordance with the Convention's provisions. However, the UN Convention has not been incorporated into domestic legislation, so the specific rights set out in it are not legally enforceable in domestic courts (Bainham 1993:607–8). The UN Convention does, however, require governments to produce reports on the progress of implementation to the UN Committee on the Rights of the Child. While the UK government produced a complacent report on compliance with the UN Convention in 1994, voluntary agencies have worked effectively to analyse the extent of compliance and continue to lobby for the Convention's effective implementation (see CRDU 1994 for a comprehensive analysis of the extent to which the UK complies with the UN Convention, and also Newell 1991).

The UK government has argued that the Children Act 1989 complies with and even goes beyond the UN Convention, so it is to the Children Act 1989 that we now turn.

Children Act 1989

The Children Act 1989, like the UN Convention, emerged following a long period of debate and deliberation drawing upon a range of sources (including public inquiries, parliament and the law commission). Again, like the UN Convention, a range of interested parties, including professional groupings and a wide range of voluntary and campaigning organisations, were involved (often successfully) in lobbying as the Bill progressed through Parliament (see Parton 1991 for a detailed history of the Act). These diverse forces are reflected in the wide-ranging and potentially contradictory provisions of the Act (see below). Nevertheless, the Act has been hailed as a major step forward for children's rights, particularly in terms of autonomy or participation rights (for example Newell 1991:xiii; Franklin 1995:3). In this section, we examine the Children Act 1989 against the four sets of rights – protection, best development, participation and non-discrimination – promoted by the UN Convention.

Rights to welfare/protection

A major concern of the Children Act 1989 is to ensure that children have a right to adequate care and protection. This is dealt with in two ways, first by requiring that the welfare of the child is the paramount consideration when courts make decisions, and second by setting out a statutory framework for child protection.

The Children Act 1989 counterpart to the UN Convention 'best interests of the child' principle is the welfare principle found in s.1(1). This section requires that, whenever courts are deciding questions of a child's care or upbringing, 'the child's welfare shall be the court's paramount consideration'. The welfare principle applies in care and emergency proceedings and disputes between parents, for example over residence or contact. The Act also sets out a 'checklist' of factors which the court must take into account in contested private (between parents) and all public proceedings. While the court can take into account other factors, the issues which it must have particular regard to are:

(a) the ascertainable wishes and feelings of the child concerned (considered in the light of his age and understanding);
(b) his physical, emotional and educational needs;
(c) the likely effect on him of any change in his circumstances;

(d) his age, sex, background and any characteristics of his which the court considers relevant;

(e) any harm which he has suffered or is at risk of suffering;

(f) how capable each of his parents, and any other person in relation to whom the court considers the question to be relevant, is of meeting his needs;

(g) the range of powers available to the court under this Act in the proceedings in question. (s.1(3))

There is a strong presumption that children are best cared for and protected within their own families. The new concept of 'parental responsibility' represents an attempt to move away from a view of children as possessions implicit in the old concept of 'parental rights'. Parental responsibility is defined as 'all the rights, duties, powers, responsibilities and authority which by law a parent of a child has in relation to the child and his property' (s.3(1)). The presumption of family care, and the right to privacy, is further reinforced by the 'minimum intervention' provision (s.1(5)), which prevents the court making orders in relation to children unless doing so would be better for the child than not doing so.

Part V of the Act concerns children's rights to protection. Local authorities have a duty to investigate if they have reasonable cause to suspect that a child is suffering, or is likely to suffer, significant harm (s.47(1)). Having investigated, the local authority can choose to take no action, to offer a range of services to the child and his or her family under Part III of the Act (see below) or to apply to the court for an Emergency Protection Order (EPO), a Child Assessment Order (CAO), a Care Order or a Supervision Order. The assessment that a child is suffering, or is likely to suffer, significant harm, is the crucial threshold criteria for making Care and Supervision Orders, CAOs and EPOs (ss.31(2); 43(1); 44(1)).

Rights to best development

The provisions in the Children Act 1989 to promote the child's right to the best development are framed far more restrictively than the child's right to protection. Access to housing, education, health and income support fall largely outside of the scope of the Children Act, although s.27 allows the local authority to request the help of agencies, including the local education authority, housing department and health authority, to provide support services under Part III of the Act. As we have seen, the Children Act, like the UN Convention, emphasises that parents are generally the best people to care for their children. This is a welcome move for children. What is less welcome is the limited role given to services to support parents' efforts to provide the best possible developmental opportunities for their children. Eekelaar (1991) has pointed out how, during the early discussion of the Children Bill, the meaning of 'parental responsibility' shifted from the responsibility of parents to act dutifully towards their children to responsibility for child care belonging to parents rather than the state. Thus, while the state recognises the importance of families to children, it has done less to recognise the importance of services to families. The care of children remains a largely individualised and privatised responsibility.

The Act does provide some assistance to support parental care of children. Great importance is placed in Guidance on working in partnership with parents and on the rights of children to have contact with parents and other family members. Part III of the Act is very important in terms of offering family support services (including day care, accommodation, after care, advice, guidance and counselling, home help and family centres). However, the general duty to provide family support services to safeguard and promote children's welfare is restricted to children who are 'in need' (s.17(1)).

As we will see in Chapter 4, while the 'in need' definition is widely defined, it tends in practice to be interpreted more narrowly. Section 17 places a duty on local authorities:

(a) to safeguard and promote the welfare of children within their area who are in need; and
(b) so far as is consistent with that duty, to promote the upbringing of such children by their families,
by providing a range and level of services appropriate to those children's needs.

In need is defined as:

(a) he is unlikely to achieve or maintain, or to have the opportunity of achieving or maintaining, a reasonable standard of health or development without the provision for him of services by a local authority under this Part;
(b) his health or development is likely to be significantly impaired, or further impaired, without the provision for him of such services; or
(c) he is disabled.   (s.17(10))

For those children deemed not 'in need', the Act therefore gives no mandate to provide family support services, although day care may be provided for under-5s who are not in need (s.18(2)). In practice, resource scarcity has meant that 'in need' has been restrictively interpreted to include the minority of children at risk associated with parenting, rather than economic, social or environmental, hazards (see Chapter 4).

Participation rights

The Children Act 1989 has been seen as a major step forward in promoting the participation rights of children. The Act as a whole favours an inclusive style of decision-making, particularly emphasising the involvement of parents as partners in decision-making. Alongside this, there is some emphasis on involving children in decisions affecting them. Bainham argues that the Act 'generally supports the notion of participatory decision-making which gives to young people a degree of self-determination. This general principle to have regard to children's views marks an important adjustment in the balance of power between children and adult society' (1993:60).

An essential backdrop to the Children Act 1989 provisions on participation rights is the landmark Gillick case (*Gillick* v. *West Norfolk and Wisbech Health Authority* [1986] AC 112). The issue in this case was whether or not it was lawful for doctors to give contraceptive advice to a girl under 16 without parental consent. The implications of the case, which was ultimately decided in the House of Lords on a majority ruling, have stretched far beyond the issue of contraception. The impact of the ruling, according to Lyon and Parton, is 'to undermine fundamentally the traditional notion of parental rights to govern children'. The parent's power is seen as a dwindling one, which the courts would hesitate to enforce against the wishes of the child, particularly as he or she grows older. Parental power begins as the power of control but ends as little more than advice. When the child is deemed competent to make the decision, when he or she has attained sufficient age and understanding, the parents' power 'yields to the child's right to make his/her own decisions' (1995:43).

What need to be clearly distinguished in the discussion are children's rights to participate (to be informed or consulted in decision-making) and children's rights to autonomy (to make decisions). As we will see, the Act greatly enhances the former but restricts the latter even for Gillick-competent children. Even the extension of rights to participate in decisions is not consistent throughout the Act. The rights accorded to children depend not only on such crucial factors as their age and maturity, but also on the issues at stake.

The Act's provisions relating to participation give children different roles and statuses:

- *Non-participants.* In some instances, children have no rights in the Act to participate in decision-making. The clearest examples are those children whose parents are divorcing or separating where the parents agree on the arrangements for their children. In uncontested private law proceedings, there is no duty on the parents or the courts to consult with the child on their preferences for residence or contact.

- *Information-receivers.* Local authorities have a duty to publish information about family support services (Schedule 2, para 2(2)). More specifically, there is an expectation that those working with children not only seek children's views, but also explain to the child any decisions made. Looked-after children, for example, who have been involved in developing a care plan and reviews, must be notified of the outcome, including, crucially, the way in which their views have been incorporated or, if there is any divergence, the reasons for this (Guidance, Volume 4, paras 2.62; 3.25).

- *Consultees.* The Act requires that the child's opinions be identified in a wide range of decisions affecting children. The 'welfare checklist' demand that courts have regard to 'the ascertainable wishes and feelings of the child concerned (considered in the light of his age and understanding)' (s.1(3)(a)) when making s.8 or Care or Supervision Orders. Local authorities have a duty to give due consideration to the views of looked-after children (again subject to age and understanding) (s.22). Similar duties are imposed on voluntary organisations (s.61(2)(3)) and children's homes (s.64(2)(3)). The extension of the guardian ad litem system in public law proceedings (s.41) and the new independent visitor system (Schedule 2, para 17) for looked-after children provide additional mechanisms for ascertaining and articulating the child's views.

Whilst the Act requires that the voice of the child be heard, it is by no means the only voice to be heard, nor will it necessarily be the one which holds sway. The rights given by the Act are generally those of consultation; the duty is to 'have regard' to the child's views, which is different from determination. The right to consultation is secondary to the paramountcy of welfare (although these will not be mutually exclusive). The weight to be given to a child's views is subject to 'age and understanding', with the expectation that more weight will be given to the views of the more mature (but not simply chronologically mature) child.

- *Consenters.* There are few areas of the Act in which children are given a right to determine the actual outcome of a decision. This takes the form of giving consent and is subject to an assessment of the child's competence to make the decision. Children are empowered by the Act to refuse a medical or psychiatric examination, assessment or treatment if deemed Gillick-competent (ss.38(6); 43(8); 44(7)) (see below for how this right has been restricted by the courts). Looked-after children may also refuse the local authority's choice of independent visitor for them (or refuse their continuing appointment), although again only if deemed of sufficient understanding to make an informed decision (Schedule 2, para 17(5)(6)).

- *Initiators.* The Children Act gives children the right to apply for leave to take their own independent legal action. Children may now seek the leave of the court to make applications for s.8 Orders (that is Contact, Residence, Specific Issues and Prohibited Steps) (s.10(8)) or to be joined as parties to the proceedings, as well as to apply for the discharge of a Care Order (s.39(1)) or the discharge or variation of a Supervision Order (s.39(2)). The court has to be satisfied only that the child has sufficient understanding to make the application and not that the welfare principle be satisfied when granting leave (White *et al.* 1995:1136). On the substantive question, however, the welfare principle remains paramount.

- *Complainants.* Children who are being looked after, or who are in need, are entitled under the Act to make representations or complaints about local authority services (s.26(3)). Voluntary organisations and registered children's homes are also required to set up complaints procedures.

So how far is the Children Act a participation charter for children? What is clear is that the extent of participatory rights depends on two key factors:

- (a) the age and understanding of the child
- (b) the issue which is at stake.

For the older competent child, the Act extends rights of consultation into rights to initiate and rights to give or withhold consent. Children who are not deemed competent will still, in many instances, be consulted and informed but will have less weight accorded to their expressed wishes and feelings. Non-Gillick-competent children cannot initiate their own applications and cannot withhold consent.

Aside from maturity, a key factor in determining participation rights is the issue at stake. Certain groups of children have more rights than others. For children for whom the quality of parenting has been questioned, and where children are being looked after, there is significantly more emphasis placed on listening to the child than in divorce/separation where, as we have seen, the presumption of parental responsibility means that the child's voice will only be heard in the minority of cases where parents disagree.

Lyon and Parton argue that the Act does represent a move towards recognising children as independent subjects rather than objects of welfare: 'Children are entitled to have a say in matters affecting them but not the final say. The provisions offer children qualified autonomy but stop well short of allowing children full consequence of action' (1995:42). Precisely what weight will be given by court and welfare professionals to children's views, and how age and understanding will be assessed, will be crucial, and it is here that paternalistic attitudes to children may undermine the provisions in the Act that make children subjects rather than objects.

Since the implementation of the Act, there have been a number of events that have indicated a continuing degree of paternalism among the judiciary and resulted in a weakening of the autonomy rights even of 'competent' children. Lyon and Parton (1995) identify a number of such moves, including a Practice Direction issued by the High Court Family Division requiring that all applications by children be immediately transferred to the High Court rather than being dealt with by county or magistrates courts (Practice Direction (Family Proceedings Order: Applications by Children) [1993] 1All ER 820). It is the case of *South Glamorgan County Council* v. *W and B* ([1992] 1 FLR 574) that causes them most concern. Here a 'Gillick-competent' 15-year-old girl had exercised her right under s.38(6) to refuse a psychiatric assessment but was overruled by the court through the exercise of the court's inherent jurisdiction. Lyon and Parton conclude rather pessimistically that, as far as the judiciary is concerned, 'many of the so-called Gillick provisions of the Children Act 1989 conferring rights upon children are in reality merely conferring strong claims for the child's voice to be heard' (1995:53).

Rights to non-discrimination

Unlike in the UN Convention, there is no explicit commitment in the Children Act 1989 that the rights given apply to all children, regardless of gender, ethnicity or disability. Instead, the thinking behind the Act reflects a belief that different groups of children will have different needs that must be taken into account by the courts and welfare professionals. Thus, rather than emphasising formal equality of treatment, which can lead to assimilationist, culturally insensitive or colour/gender-blind approaches, there is a focus on identifying and meeting the specific needs of individual children (Macdonald 1991).

In terms of culture and ethnicity, much emphasis is placed on ensuring that those who are providing care for children should be sensitive towards the child's specific heritage. A duty is placed on local authorities to give 'due consideration' to 'the child's religious persuasion, racial origin and cultural and linguistic background' when making decisions about looked after children (s.22(5)(c)). A similar duty is placed on voluntary organisations accommodating children (s.61(3)(c)) and registered children's homes (64(3)(c)). Local authorities are required to consider the different racial groups to which children in need belong when arranging for the provision of day care or when recruiting foster carers (Schedule 2, para 11). Day care providers may be deregistered if the care provided is seriously inadequate in relation to the child's needs, with a specific reference to the need to take into account a child's religious persuasion, racial origin and cultural and linguistic background (s.74).

It is surprising that ethnicity and religion are not specifically mentioned in the 'welfare checklist', an omission that has caused some concern (Macdonald 1991). The inclusion of 'age, sex, background and any characteristics of his which the court considers relevant (s.1(3)) does, however, enable the court to consider a range of factors which could include ethnicity and cultural background'.

The Act contains a number of provisions requiring local authorities to provide services for children with disabilities. Children with disabilities are automatically defined as children in need under s.17. Local authorities are also required to establish a register of disabled children as a means to plan service provision (Schedule 2, para 2). Local authorities are also required to provide services:

(a) to minimize the effect on disabled children within their area of their disabilities; and

(b) to give such children the opportunity to lead lives which are as normal as possible.   (Schedule 2, para 6)

Mixed messages: rights in practice

It would be wrong, however, to assume that we have moved slowly but inexorably to a position where children's rights are always at the centre of decision-making. The picture is far more complex than a slow shift from *laissez-faire* to state paternalism to parent's rights and children's rights. In many ways, the Children Act 1989 reflects aspects of all four of Fox Harding's child care perspectives, not always coexisting in harmony (Kaganas *et al.* 1995). Over the past century, the family has come to accept interference from the state as an ordinary part of everyday life, through state regulation of education, health and safety. Scrutiny now exists not only in relation to normal health and development outside the home at school, but also within the home about the bounds of reasonable parenting. A difficult balance must be struck throughout between autonomy and regulation, between recognising families as responsible for both causing and resolving problems. As Bell notes:

> The contemporary situation is one in which the family is regarded as autonomous, and craves that autonomy from outside interference, whilst at the same time being subject to regulation by norms that guard against its possible arbitrariness. (Bell 1993:392)

At the beginning of this chapter, we identified how variable are understandings of 'children' and 'childhood'. We emphasised how these ideas change over time, and how these have related to different child care policies. Both Fox Harding (1991) and Freeman (1992) concur that the Children Act 1989 contains a heady and potentially contradictory mix of principles, combining paternalism with partnership with parents and children's rights. As Freeman notes:

> The presence of such different ideologies suggests the conflicts of the 1980s have not truly been resolved, that divisions were papered over and that, not far below the surface, conflict remains. (1992:4)

As Freeman (1992:5) points out, what is crucial is how these potentially contradictory principles and broad frameworks are worked out in practice. Agency policies, professional practice and parental support are crucial to translating the range of rights accorded to children in the UN Convention and the Children Act 1989 into a reality. We will focus on how practitioners can support the development of children's rights in practice in the following chapters, but it is worth pausing briefly to illustrate just how complex working with rights can be in practice.

CASE STUDY

Three siblings, Sarah aged 10, Peter aged 6 and David aged 4, all need long-term placement. All three children have the same mother, who is white British, and different fathers. Sarah's father is black (black British, African Caribbean origins). The two boys have white British fathers.

The social worker began to ascertain the children's wishes and feelings and was told by the 10-year-old that she wanted to be placed separately from her siblings. The two boys did not appear to have any clear views on being with their sister. Two separate placements were sought on the basis of this. When a new social worker became involved and spoke with the children again, she learnt of the 10-year-old's distress at being separated from her siblings. Sarah had spoken to the previous social worker only once, the day after a row with her brothers.

This case illustrates some of the complexities of balancing different types of rights. It poses dilemmas for social workers about how the different types of rights Sarah has can be balanced, between the rights to have a say in major decisions about her life and the right to have her welfare safeguarded. However, it also raises questions about whose rights should prevail when the rights of different individuals are in conflict, in this case between Sarah's rights and those of her siblings. Additionally, the case illustrates the importance of building up a relationship with a child over some time, rather than relying on a single brief encounter, to get to understand the child, her wishes and feelings and the context of her life. The issues of 'race' and gender in this case add further complications. The temptation for the worker is to simply 'hear' Sarah's expressed wish to be placed separately as her self-identification with her separate racial heritage or, alternatively, on the basis of her sex.

Conclusion

In this chapter, we have set out the context of social work with children. In doing so, we have emphasised the dynamic and changing context of child care policy and practice. At the present time, the legal framework presents a more 'balanced' approach to children and family, combining participation and protection, non-discrimination and best development. The difficulty, or the challenge, for social workers is that the balancing act is often in their hands. As Sarah's case demonstrates, this will require much skill, commitment and time to achieve. In Part Two of this book, we will examine in much more detail how social workers can address these dilemmas in practice.

Further reading

Brannen, J. and O'Brien, M. (eds) (1996) *Children in Families: Research and Policy* (Brighton: Falmer Press).

This book of edited chapters is a guide to current issues in the sociology of childhood, in and beyond the UK, that have practical applications for practitioners. The focus on children as subjects of research offers techniques that could be adapted for use in social work practice with children.

Children's Rights Development Unit (1994) *UK Agenda for Children* (London: CRDU).

A comprehensive analysis of the extent to which UK law and policy complies with the UN Convention. It contains a vast amount of information on a wide range of issues, including day care, adoption, poverty and homelessness.

Franklin, B. (ed.) (1995) *The Handbook of Children's Rights* (London: Routledge).

A collection of articles analysing the legal framework of children's rights, policy initiatives and international perspectives on children's rights.

Harding, L. Fox (1991) *Perspectives in Child Care Policy* (Harlow: Longman).

An original analysis identifying four perspectives that have been influential in British child care policy up to the present day.

Parton, N. (1991) *Governing the Family: Child Care, Child Protection and the State* (Basingstoke: Macmillan).

This provides a detailed context to contemporary social work and the state's role in family life, looking in particular at the influence of child abuse enquiries.

2

Age and Understanding: The Developmental Framework

Introduction

When social workers are observing, talking to, listening to or playing with children, they need to have the knowledge and skills to take into account the developmental processes of childhood and, specifically, children's own changing perspective on their world. The child must be seen as an actor in his or her own life rather than just a passive recipient of parenting and other experiences. From birth, the child will be trying to *make sense* of the world and will construct a framework for understanding and responding to events and relationships. Social workers need to be constantly asking, what is the child's experience of this situation? What does it mean to them? The child has not only the right, but also the psychological and emotional need, to be treated as a person rather than an object of concern. In order for social workers to appreciate the experiences of children and enable them most effectively to express their wishes and feelings, they need to understand a child's view of the world in its developmental context.

In the welfare check list (s.1.3) and throughout the Children Act 1989, the expression 'according to the child's age and understanding' is used as a test for determining how much weight should be given to a child's wishes and feelings when decisions are made.

Decision-making, however, is only part of the picture. Social workers in all aspects of their face-to-face work with children, whether for brief assessment or in relationship-based work, need to be able to make sense of children's *understanding* of their world. The nature of the child's understanding relates to age, developmental stage, experiences and the different family and social contexts of the child's world. For the social worker, the child's age and stage will have implications for the kind of work to follow. With babies and very young children, the social worker will be learning to see the world through the particular child's eyes by direct observation of and

37

collecting information about the child's behaviour. As children get older, they will communicate through play, drawing, speech and writing. The social worker needs to put all these communications in the context of the child's development. We begin therefore by considering some ways of defining development before looking in more detail at each age and stage.

What do we mean by child development?

The concept of child development itself is usually subdivided into a number of categories. For the purpose of social work practice, it is helpful to think of development in terms of the categories used in the Children Act – *physical, emotional, behavioural, intellectual* and *social* development – because these are the categories that need to be considered when a child is deemed to be in need or at risk of significant harm. It is important to remember, however, that, although these areas of development can be separated out in order to ensure that the worker has a comprehensive picture of a child's developmental state, it soon becomes apparent that all areas of development are interconnected. The development of language and communication skills, for example, will rely on *cognitive, emotional* and *social* development. *Physical health* and *emotional well-being* will affect the ability both to concentrate and to maximise *intellectual* achievement. The separation of the various strands in order to appreciate the different potential areas of concern when working with a child must therefore be linked with an understanding of the complex connections.

The other categories of which social workers need to be very much aware are the dimensions identified in the 'Looking After Children' system for assessing and planning for children looked after by the local authority:

- health
- education
- identity
- family and social relationships
- social presentation
- emotional and behavioural development
- self-care skills.

These areas of development are wider than those included in the tests of need or harm in the Children Act 1989 and are designed to enable detailed assessments to be made which link children's development to the quality of care they are receiving. Care in this context is expected to include paying attention to aspects of children's lives outside the home, such as education. Although the 'Looking After Children' materials have been most fully developed with a view to improving the care of children in foster and residential care, they are likely to be useful in a range of assessment situations, which will in turn better inform the worker's face-to-face work with the child.

In the beginning: the first year of life

Primary tasks: developing trust and a sense of security; forming attachments

Even on a purely physical level, there will be differences in the quality of a child's start in life. The mother's well-being, diet and access to antenatal care during pregnancy will affect the unborn child. Poverty and poor health affect the likelihood of problems during pregnancy and at birth. In more serious cases, drug misuse can lead to the baby suffering withdrawal symptoms, and excessive alcohol intake by the mother may lead to what is known as fetal alcohol syndrome. Such pre-birth factors may affect a number of aspects of development. Babies born with fetal alcohol syndrome, for example, have physical problems such as heart defects, as well as cognitive problems such as learning difficulties, and behavioural problems such as poor concentration. In the USA, fetal alcohol syndrome is the leading cause of learning disabilities in children, exceeding the rate from Down's syndrome (Streissguth *et al.* 1991). Awareness of such risks needs to be accompanied by good observational skills to establish how these babies then develop in the context of the care they receive in their families.

The baby is born with its senses alert for the experience of the most important part of the environment – other human beings who are going to meet the need for food, for warmth and touch, for special smells, for reassuring sounds and smiles. Newborn babies have quite sophisticated perceptual skills and are able to discriminate between their mother and others by sight, sound and smell from only a few days old – and to indicate a preference for their own mother. Such abilities demonstrate the way in which, from the beginning, babies have the capacity to form special relationships.

The possibility that relationships will form relies not only on the baby's capacities but also on the response of the available adults. The nature of the feeling which the parent has for the baby from birth is usually referred to as bonding. Klaus and Kennell (1976) argue, on the basis of their research, that there is a critical time immediately after the birth when the mother must start to bond with the baby. Subsequent research (reviewed by Sluckin *et al.* 1983) challenged this instant, 'superglue' model of bonding and suggested that the development of a parent's feeling for a child is a gradual process that does not necessarily require immediate physical closeness after the birth. What appears to be more likely is that the time after birth should be seen as a sensitive rather than a critical time for the parent's feelings toward the child to develop. Mothers engage in this process and so also do fathers (Bee 1997). There are a certain number of instances of bonding failure, when mothers feel indifferent or even hostile towards their baby. In the most severe cases, this needs highly intensive intervention in order to establish a bonding relationship before the baby becomes avoidant of the mother. Once the baby starts to turn away from the mother, the mother is likely to find it even more difficult to establish a relationship.

The sensitivity of the child to the messages she receives about the world is a very significant area for child care social workers. From the early weeks, babies react differently to the mother's expressions of happiness, sadness or anger (Haviland and Lelwica 1987). The mother's facial expression of emotions will also affect the baby's ability to play with toys (Harris 1989:23). Social workers need to be aware of the implication of these research findings for children who receive confusing or negative emotional cues, perhaps from parents who are depressed or preoccupied. Children who witness domestic violence will also be receiving messages that will encourage them to fear or distrust the environment in which they find themselves. Social workers have often underestimated the consequences of such aspects of children's environments (Brandon and Lewis 1996).

Attachment

Bowlby's work on attachment theory (1969, 1979, 1980) has made a major contribution to how social workers think about the development of relationships between children and parents. Attachment is a central concept in social work practice with children because it is most often in the area of children's close family relationships that we see the origins of emotional and behavioural problems. For social workers, it is also important to understand the links between attachment and abusive and neglectful parenting (Crittendon and Ainsworth 1989).

Attachment theory specifically addresses three areas of behaviour in children:

- *Proximity-seeking.* The child seeks to remain within reach of a protective parent or other attachment figure, especially when feeling anxious or under threat.
- *The secure base effect.* Over time, the predictable availability of the attachment figure allows the child to feel secure enough to explore, play and learn.
- *Separation protest.* The child will protest if access to the attachment figure is denied.

Most children are, by the age of 6–8 months, likely to be showing a strong preference for a particular adult who provides a secure emotional base, although we know that, even during this early phase, children can form a number of attachment relationships. The importance of the secure base effect in facilitating learning is a key factor in social and intellectual development in young children. Children develop the ability to explore their environment confident in the knowledge that the attachment figure will be there if needed. This process frees the child to learn about the world in which she finds herself. The emotional security also allows the child to use her energies in order to learn and grow rather than be preoccupied with anxiety. What is more, Bowlby argued, the pattern of relating develops into an 'internal working model'. The child has a model of self, others and the relationship between them (Howe 1995) that carries over into future relationships inside and outside the family. This may include the relationship between the child and the social worker. For the social worker observing or working directly with a child, it will be the detail and the pattern of relationships that will give clues to the child's internal working model. Examination of the child's behaviour and interactions allows the social worker to assess the child's model of the world around her in more sophisticated way.

For social workers, one of the most useful ways in which attachment formation has been described is in Vera Fahlberg's work. Fahlberg (1988) describes the process of forming a secure attachment as a cycle that relies on the parent being sensitive to the signals of the child when she communicates physical or psychological needs.

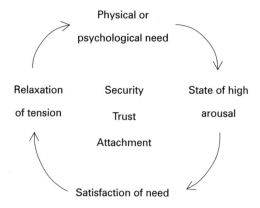

Figure 2.1   Arousal–relaxation cycle

These cycles reflect what are the earliest forms of 'conversation', leading to synchronicity between adult and child. The expression of need and sensitive responses, followed by the relaxation of tension, forms a predictable rhythm or pattern. Out of the repetition of such cycles over time comes the child's sense of *trust* in the predictability of the parent and the use of the parent as a secure base, someone who can be relied on to be available physically and emotionally, the 'good enough' parent, as Winnicott (1965) put it. Observation of these relationship patterns in the first year of life allows social workers to be alert to what may be going wrong in the early stages of emotional development, but the cycles can also be used throughout childhood as a way of making sense of parent–child relationships and identifying difficulties. A state of high arousal where needs are not met, for example, may be a crying baby, a toddler having a tantrum or a teenager who is out of control. When parenting is neglectful or rejecting, young children may cease to communicate needs. When babies are extremely neglected from birth, they may be fretful and cry a great deal initially, but they are quite rapidly likely to become extremely passive, quiet and flat emotionally. They may sleep for much of the day and not demand to be fed. A 'good' baby who fails to gain weight must be carefully observed and assessed.

The parent or carer should also be initiating interactions, which give children positive feelings about themselves (Fahlberg 1988).

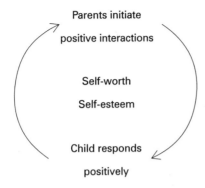

Figure 2.2   The cycle of positive interactions

Where children are not experiencing positive interactions with parents or carers, their self-esteem suffers. Social workers may find that, for children who have experienced a lack of responsiveness to expressed needs as in the first cycle, offers of kindness or positive comments are not trusted and the social worker offering them is rejected. Foster carers also find this, and it may prove frustrating for them that a child who comes from an adverse family environment appears not to appreciate good care when it is offered. The cycle leading to trust and attachment needs to develop first.

Separation anxiety and models of attachment

Much of the development of attachment theory has relied on considering the impact of separation and the nature of separation anxiety. As Bowlby put it:

> Attachment theory is a way of conceptualising the propensity of human beings to make strong affectional bonds to particular others and of explaining the many forms of emotional distress and personality disturbance, including anxiety, anger, depression and emotional detachment, to which unwilling separation and loss give rise. (Bowlby 1979:127)

Since Bowlby's original formulation of attachment theory, there have been a number of developments that use the effect of separation as a method for determining the *quality* of attachments. Mary Ainsworth developed a method of classifying patterns of secure and insecure attachment relationships (Ainsworth *et al.* 1979). She used an experimental setting, referred to as the 'Strange situation', to examine how children reacted differently to brief separations from mothers and reacted to strangers. The classification defines secure attachment and three categories of insecure attachment: detached/ avoidant, resistant/ambivalent and disorganised/disoriented. These models require detailed consideration (see Howe 1995) and, for social workers working with individual children, it is helpful to have an understanding of the evidence of the quality of a child's attachments. A child who is very clingy to a mother, for example, may be demonstrating an insecure attachment, while a child who plays contentedly and only occasionally turns to her mother may have a secure attachment. These are not always easy distinctions to make, and it is helpful to think about these behaviours as defensive strategies. As Howe has pointed out:

> the behaviour of insecurely attached children is an adaptive response within the context of the relationship in which they find themselves. The behaviour adopted is a defensive strategy developed by the child in order to cope with feelings of anxiety, uncertainty and fear. (1995: 89)

In the first year of life, children are learning very fast about the world in which they live and about their place within it. Although there has always been some dispute about the extent to which these very early experiences determine the child's route through life, and clearly subsequent events can and do have a major influence, early experiences are undoubtedly very important in laying the foundation of some of the child's basic skills and patterns of relationships.

Age and understanding in the first year

- Babies are born with different constitutions, personalities and temperaments. They *not only react to, but also interact with* carers, siblings and professionals.

- Babies are extremely sensitive to their carers and all aspects of their environment. They *communicate* their feeling states by their facial expressions, moods and behaviour and also in other ways, such as the pattern of weight gain, meeting developmental milestones and so on.

- The importance of *attachment formation* during this year will mean that there needs to be a careful observation and assessment of attachment behaviours and relationships with carers. Knowledge of early experiences can be helpful in putting older children's behaviour in context. The theoretical framework regarding insecure attachments is important in making sense of apparently contradictory or defensive reactions in children.

Pre-school children

Primary tasks: moving from dependency to autonomy; communicating with language; learning to play; early social development

If the major task of the first year is to develop trust and attachment, the years from 1 to 3 see the child moving from dependency to establishing a degree of autonomy. Autonomy in this sense does not mean total control but it does mean the child making choices within the safe boundaries of the environment. As Fahlberg says, parents at this stage need to respond to the child in whatever way will make the child feel more capable (1994:67). This is often the age of contradictions. As the process of psychological separation begins, the child may experience anxiety about physical separation and will need to make greater use of the attachment figure as a secure base or may become very clingy. The 20-month-old child who is one day demanding the freedom to choose what to wear, may the next day demand to be spoon-fed.

Part of the tension between dependency and autonomy tends to express itself in defiant and negative behaviour in this age group. Dunn's research (1988:15) found that the majority of 2–3-year-olds persisted in demands or did what they had just been told not to do. This process of assertiveness is an appropriate part of establishing oneself as a separate, autonomous person with ideas of one's own. It also becomes a way of testing out the limits and boundaries that the adult world, initially the parents, is going to impose. For certain parents, the defiant toddler represents a challenge to their authority that they are unable to tolerate. Parents will draw heavily on their own childhood experiences of being parented, and if this was harsh or neglectful, they may find it impossible to sustain a loving relationship with a child whom they see as powerful or hostile. The parent may blame the child for being a constitutionally difficult child, and the normal assertiveness of the child may be experienced as persecutory, as being deliberately hurtful to the parent. In extreme cases, this will lead to rejection or exclusion of the child by shutting her in a bedroom or to attempts to control the child by physical punishment. Research has shown that where the child experiences persistently negative responses, the child becomes even more stressed and is more persistently negative to the parents (Bugental *et al.* 1989). Where parents are unpredictable and punitive, the child can appear to be frozen and be physically immobilised by anxiety. Watchfulness, yet avoiding eye contact, may prove to be the best way for the child to anticipate and avoid parental rejection. Of course, this kind of strategy means that the child will not develop trust, will have a poor self-esteem and will not have energy available to explore the environment and learn.

Language development

Language is such a critical part of development at this stage that it merits special attention. As with other areas of development, there is a wide range of ages within which it is normal to develop language skills. Some children, for example, use a number of individual words at 8 months, others not until 18 months. Some use two-word sentences at 18 months, while others may not do so until at least 2 years of age. Social workers will need to consult with speech therapists in order to make reasonable judgements about language development, but observations in the family setting will allow them to get a fuller picture of the child's level and style of communication.

Parents who provide a stimulating language environment, by talking to the child, reading to the child, eliciting language from the child and then responding contingently, help children to develop language. Children who are growing up in relatively chaotic households, where language is rarely directed specifically at children, apart from instructions, are more likely to experience difficulties. This is particularly the case where the reciprocal and synchronous relationship described above in relation to attachment formation has not developed during infancy, so that the pattern of conversation is missing from the child's repertoire. It must also be the case that children communicate in language when this appears to be a successful way of getting needs met. If attempts at language are not met positively, other forms of behaviour that gain attention, such as screaming or having tantrums, are more likely to occur. Whatever the cause, children who are unable to use language to communicate can be seriously disadvantaged in all areas of development.

Play and social learning

The young child's ability to play enables her both to explore physical relationships, that is how many bricks can balance in a tower, and then to move on to use wooden bricks as symbols for sweets or cars. The next step is socio-dramatic play in which the child learns to role-play a parent feeding the child or getting cross, and in this way she safely explores social situations. The pre-school child needs to learn not only about the relationships in which she herself is involved, but also about all kinds of relationships between others if she is to be a sophisticated operator in the social world. She needs to learn about how people feel and think, and then use this knowledge to understand why people behave in the way they do. This capacity has important survival value for the child. She needs to know how to read not only her parents, but also other adults and other children, inside and outside the family, in order to understand what is going on, the impact this will have on her and the ways in which to get her needs met.

This complex area has attracted considerable research, which has been able to demonstrate that children's grasp of the subtleties of 'other minds' can become quite accomplished quite early on. Judy Dunn's research found that, by the age of 3, children were demonstrating an understanding of other's feelings:

> the causes of pain, distress, anger, pleasure and displeasure, comfort and fear in others as well as themselves. They joke, play with, and tell stories about these feeling states in self and other. (Dunn 1988:170)

Out of this understanding comes what she describes as 'the foundations for the moral virtues of caring, considerateness and kindness'.

This area of learning, as with most others at this age, will depend on the quality of the family environment. It depends on the parents being able to communicate to the child about their adult feeling states and to help the child communicate about her own by putting feelings into words. Some parents, often because of their own experience of parenting or at times because of current problems such as depression, do not engage in this process. Although they may have conversations with their young children, those conversations are limited in the extent to which they help the child to explore feelings and learn about the complexities of the social world. For some pre-school children, the social worker's language and use of materials, such as sad, angry, or happy faces, may seem like a foreign language, which they simply do not understand. Similarly, these children's capacity to use imaginative play with dolls to recreate social situations may be very limited.

During the pre-school years, the continuing development of autonomy and individuation is then put in the context of learning about right and wrong. The child of this age is developing more of a sense of what she ought to be doing and what is acceptable as pro-social behaviour. Alongside this comes the development of the child's sense of self-esteem and the wish to please others. How the child values and judges herself will be linked to the way in which she is valued and judged by others. During the pre-school period, children are conscious not only of the value placed on them, but also of the role they have to play in pleasing adults and winning their approval. Although most children receive, on balance, positive messages about themselves, for children who find that whatever they do they are not able to win parental approval, it is likely that lessons about appropriate behaviour, necessary for them to cope with peers and at school, will not be learned. Often in the context of children's insecure attachments, children's behaviour can effectively provoke the very abuse or rejection they most fear, but at least it is then predictable.

What is often overlooked is the importance of peer group and sibling relationships in this age group. Dunn's (1993) work has demonstrated the complexity of relationships between children and has, to that extent, challenged the exclusive emphasis on attachment relationships with parents. For social workers, this research is important if only because many young children who are causing concern within their families are also not having the opportunity to play with other children and learn skills or benefit from peer relationships. It also suggests that when, working with children, it is important to acknowledge the role that friends and siblings play.

Finally, it is important to clarify our thinking about the three elements often associated with this age group: egocentrism, omnipotence and magical thinking. Because of their research evidence of young children's capacity for empathy and social understanding, Dunn and other researchers have questioned Piaget's notion that young children are by nature egocentric. However, it seems useful to distinguish between the child's capacity to understand that others have their own perspective and the child's capacity to take the perspectives of others into account in their own actions. As described above, children who have experienced parenting in which parents are unpredictable, inconsistent and rarely share their feelings explicitly with their children may not have taught children how to understand other minds. Sometimes the child simply learns to anticipate a parent's reactions, as many abused children learn to do in order to avoid further hurt. However, this does not help the child in developing constructive responses to other adults or children. What is more, if a child is preoccupied with getting her own needs met, she may not be able to take account of or give priority to the perspective or the feelings of others in her behaviour. In this sense, even if the child has the cognitive ability to understand the feelings of others, she is egocentric in the broader sense of not being emotionally able to translate this into action. She may continue to assault her younger sister and take her toy even though she knows it is painful to her sister and that the toy is important to her.

It is also the case that children who face stressful situations are often egocentric in the sense of seeing themselves as responsible for what has happened to them. This feeling of omnipotence, which is often linked to what is known as 'magical thinking', can be particularly overwhelming for children between the ages of 4 and 7 or 8, who are still trying to make sense of their own world (Jewett 1994). Social workers need to be on the alert for the ways in which children blame themselves for the separation of parents, for parental illness and for the abuse which they have experienced. For example:

Dad became ill and went to hospital because I was naughty.

My little brother got taken into care because I hit him.

In the enquiry into the death of Sukina, aged 5, the report comments on the fact that just before she lost consciousness after being assaulted, she said, 'I'm sorry daddy' (Stone 1991). The child who smiles to placate an unpredictable parent or the child who blames herself for her own ill-treatment may not react in a way that makes sense in commonsense terms. Spending time with children needs to be accompanied by knowledge of children's reactions to abuse.

Magical thinking may also be connected with the tendency for the pre-school child to have a vivid fantasy life. Fear of the dark is the most common fear for children of this age, and ideas about monsters and evil figures may feature quite strongly. This may be concretely expressed by a child's preoccupation with specific figures from horror films. For some children, fantasies of evil can be linked with threatening adults but may also be linked with their sense of their own capacity to do harm.

Age and understanding

- Children of pre-school age are negotiating a significant phase in their emotional development. How children relate to attachment figures, how they cope with separation anxiety, how they relate to other children, how they relate to you the social worker, will all communicate information about aspects of their *emotional well-being*.

- Where pre-school children have had positive experiences of parenting, they should also have developed *a good sense of self* and have a *satisfactory level of self-esteem*. This is a period of learning, enthusiasm and interest in the world. Where there are insecure attachments, children are likely to demonstrate avoidance or ambivalence/preoccupation, especially around separations. They will also demonstrate a lack of confidence in new situations or in tackling unfamiliar tasks.

- Children who have experienced reasonably predictable, responsive and stimulating parenting will have developed the ability to *play* and to *communicate using language*. Children who have not had this experience are likely to need extra help to communicate their feelings.

- Issues of *security and control* remain critical. Children who have been given clear boundaries will have learned to live within the norms of their family and to some extent of the outside world. Where parents have been unavailable, unpredictable or rejecting, children may feel and may be out of control. The high level of anxiety and acting-out behaviour that this generates in children will make it difficult to contain them. It may also make it difficult for them to articulate their feelings.

- Even very vulnerable and disturbed pre-school children need to be listened to and can, with help, communicate. They are likely to be finding it very hard to make sense of their situation, both cognitively and emotionally. The complex mix of anxiety, fantasy and magical thinking, in addition to the wide range of verbal and non-verbal forms of communication at this age, has implications for the skills needed to ascertain a child's wishes and feelings.

Primary school children

Primary tasks: developing a sense of self in relation to the outside world; learning the rules

Bentovim (1972) once put it that, by the age of 5, a child needs many of the qualities required for adult life:

- to be emotionally ready to learn
- to have a clear idea of herself as a person
- to have the ability to relate to other children
- to have the ability to control and postpone urgent needs
- to have the ability to use initiative to find gratification in play and activities that are socially acceptable.

It is often at the point that the child enters school that deficits in these areas of development, which may have gone unaddressed in the home, become a barrier to learning and appropriate development in the primary school years. Although the period from 5 to 11 years of age does not see changes as dramatic as those from birth to 5 years of age and during adolescence, there is no question that there are significant tasks to be achieved during this period and that there can be significant problems for primary-age children when developmental difficulties arise. We know, for example, that one research study showed the highest breakdown rate for children in foster care to be among 5–11-year-olds (Berridge and Cleaver,1987).

For many reasons, this is both a challenging and rewarding age group for social workers to work with. During middle childhood, children can be much more cautious about revealing their thoughts and fears. The very fact that they are of an age to understand more of the implications of confiding about bullying to a teacher or talking about family problems to a stranger may lead to a certain reticence. However, it can often be the case that children in this age group who have been struggling to make sense of difficult experiences, perhaps of separation and loss or of maltreatment, are very much in need of someone to help them but have not found anyone to listen to them. We know, for example, that adopted children of this age will be asking questions about their family of origin (Brodzinsky *et al.* 1992). We also know that children whose parents have mental health problems or learning difficulties may have taken on a great deal of responsibility for their parents even during the primary school years and may not have had their concerns listened to. It is important not to underestimate the need for children of this age to understand what is happening around them and to them – and not to underestimate their capacity to do so if appropriate help is offered. Even when social workers have been able to build a relationship of trust with a child, professionals involved in decision-making can be rather dubious about the role that the wishes and feelings of primary-age children should have in influencing the difficult choices to be made. So workers need to be able to defend the right and the ability of children of this age to make their own contribution.

One of the central features of this period, both at school and in the family, is the nature of the developing *self-concept*. Collins (1984) suggested that there are four key tasks in the development of self-concept in middle childhood:

- developing a relatively stable and comprehensive understanding of the self
- refining one's understanding of how the social world works
- developing standards and expectations of one's own behaviour
- developing strategies for controlling or managing one's behaviour.

These tasks represent an important part of developing an identity, learning to fit in and be accepted: defining oneself in terms of a particular gender, ethnic group, class or culture, and learning what is expected of a 6-year-old living in a particular family, attending a particular school in a particular country. Racial identity in particular is becoming well established at this age (Maxime 1986), and gender stereotypes become more fixed (Williams and Best 1990). Although there will be some things that are universal, perhaps the socialisation process itself, most features will be culturally specific. In more individualistic Western cultures, children are expected to pursue individual fulfilment, albeit within certain limitations set out by society. In other cultures, it may be seen as desirable for individuals to learn to value the family or the community first and foremost. Self-esteem then depends on the contribution made to the family rather than to one's own personal goals. Having learned what is expected, the child then needs to learn how to control her impulses or moderate her behaviour in order to fit in.

Part of this process within this age group is the increasing importance of peer group relationships. Although, as Dunn (1993) has suggested, peer group relationships are important in the pre-school period, it is at school that the skills of the child in making friends and negotiating conflicts become important. Of course, not all children will have the same kinds of pattern of friendship, and it is necessary to consider the individual child very closely before drawing conclusions. Some children may be described as shy but have been found to genuinely enjoy their own company and, although possessing the skills to make relationships, are quite content with relatively loose friendships (Asendorpf 1993). Nevertheless, for many children, the need to be liked and be part of the group is very intense. The issues relating to a sense of self and standards of behaviour are relevant here, as also are some of the skills in reading others' minds. Research (Dodge *et al.* 1984) has suggested that children who are popular are more skilled at reading the intentions of others and can therefore react more appropriately. One of the most damaging aspects of the failure to read emotions and intentions is the tendency to see a hostile intention when there is none. Social workers need to be aware that this tendency is particularly associated with children who have been neglected or rejected within their families (Dodge and Feldman 1990). When children's emotional welfare is being considered, their social development in relation to peer group relationships will be central. When social workers work with children to explore their relationships, the focus needs to include their peer group relationships.

Managing anxiety and sustaining attachment relationships continue to be important through this period. Children's attachment relationships and their behaviour in the pre-school period will have developed as a strategy for adapting to their family circumstances and coping with their anxiety. Children who arrive at school age with insecure attachments and a very poor sense of boundaries to their behaviour may be extremely anxious in this new and challenging environment. Many children will react briefly by regressing, perhaps by occasional enuresis or infrequent bouts of aggressive behaviour, but will then settle if the school offers a sensitive and containing environment. For children who may have, for example, experienced more actively rejecting or ambivalent relationships at home, or have experienced emotional or sexual abuse, or been disciplined by being isolated, the anxiety may be overwhelming and difficult to contain. Some of these children will shut off entirely, which means that their anxiety and anger is under control but they will not learn. Others may react in a panic with very extreme aggression, assaulting children and teachers, particularly when there is a change in the class teacher or a change of routine. Although the behaviour is aggressive, it is important to be aware that it is the underlying anxiety that leads to the disintegration of the child's coping mechanisms. It may, for example, feed the child's fantasy that she is a powerful, evil child, who cannot be contained. As Richman's research (Richman *et al.* 1982) has suggested, severe behaviour problems in 3-year-olds are likely to persist into the primary school years, and it is not surprising that the behaviour of the out-of-control 6- or 7-year-old can seem quite similar to that of the out-of-control toddler. Such children give confused messages in their behaviour and are rarely able to put feelings into words without help or emotional and physical containment.

Children who start school from a firm basis, both emotionally and socially, will move relatively smoothly into the formal school environment. Children who are vulnerable, because of living in adversity or who have a learning or physical disability, may find the transition to school and development over the primary school period more stressful. However, for some children from difficult family backgrounds, school becomes a safe haven that can meet some of their needs for boundaries and for self-esteem. Success at school can be a protective factor in this sense, and school staff can provide a 'secure base'. For children in this position, it will be particularly important that, whatever interventions occur in relation to the child's living arrangements, continuity at school should be seen as potentially as significant as continuity *in an attachment relationship*.

Age and understanding

- Children continue to need secure emotional relationships within the family to sustain them and to offer partiality. Self-esteem is a key factor in emotional well-being.

- Peer groups are valued, and there can be a correspondingly great fear of being different, of rejection or of bullying.

- Children of primary school age, particularly aged 8–11, are wanting to know how and why things happen but often do not have the opportunity to clarify their confusion, hopes and fears. Social workers need to take the initiative rather than waiting for children to ask, particularly when children appear to be unable to put feelings into words. With help, children in this age group are able to explore their wishes and feelings about their situation. These can contribute significantly to decisions that are to be made about them without leaving them with the responsibility for decisions that are made.

Adolescence

Tasks: identity; sexuality; independence/interdependence

The boundaries of adolescence are not easy to define. It begins effectively at puberty, which is variable in itself, but its course and ending is likely to be determined by cultural factors as variable as the school-leaving age and the point at which children achieve independent adult status. As most commentators now suggest, the traditional anxiety among parents and professionals about the turbulence of adolescence is not borne out by the facts (Nielsen 1987; Herbert 1997). Although adolescence is undoubtedly a time of change and transition, it is not, for the majority of young people, necessarily associated with stress and emotional turmoil. However, what social workers will be aware of is that there is a minority of young people, particularly those who do not have firm emotional, educational and social foundations from earlier in their childhood, for whom the teenage years can throw up a number of significant difficulties, causing distress to them and concern to society. These are the 'troubled and troublesome' young people who require a considerable amount of time, energy and commitment from social workers who wish to work with them.

There are a number of different approaches to thinking about the tasks of adolescence. The physical changes of puberty are accompanied by changing expectations within families and schools and from society at large. The teenage years bring increased freedom but also increased responsibility for one's own behaviour. In our society, the gap between physical adult maturity and becoming an adult socially is wider than ever. There is an expectation that increasing numbers will remain in education beyond the age of 18 and that many young people will live with their parents into their 20s. This leads to an uncertain period of overlap between child and adult roles.

Both biological and social changes contribute to what is most commonly seen to be the major task of adolescence – the establishment of an identity. Erikson's model (1968) defines this period as a moratorium between childhood and adulthood: a new identity must be found which will place the young person in adult roles. Erikson believed that a young person searched for an ideology and that adult identity was based on this commitment. We can think of ideology in terms of a young person's search for something to believe in, something to make sense of one's life. The belief may be based on something as simple as loyalty to a particular community or cultural group. It may be a core value, such as the importance of work or the sense of a family life, which shapes one's life and structures one's choices.

For some young people, the achievement of identity is more complicated than for others. For young mothers who have had their babies while still of school age, research suggests that they negotiate simultaneously between the different identities of childhood, adolescence and adulthood (Schofield 1994). Young mothers might be breastfeeding while thinking about their GCSE coursework or phoning the housing department while squabbling with a younger brother.

For young people looked after by the local authority, the issue of identity in adolescence can be a particularly complex one. Although it is now well known that young people, whether in foster care or adopted, benefit from understanding their history and being aware of their families of origin, in most cases by having direct contact with them, many young people have lost touch with family members over the years. Even those who have contact with family members may not have a clear sense of what has happened in their lives. Many young people are able to develop a positive sense of themselves from their attachments within substitute families, but the process of negotiation is clearly not an easy one. Their sense of self will rely, of course, not only on knowledge of the past, but also on their feelings about it. Where teenagers have felt rejected or have been physically or sexually abused, the damage they take into adult life will be considerable. In spite of this, adolescents leave care at a relatively early age when other young people are continuing to receive nurturance and support from their families. Given that the normal developmental pathway is to build on existing relationships in adolescence rather than replacing them, we need to develop a model of *interdependence* rather than *independence* to ensure that the most vulnerable adolescents get the help and continuity they need.

Peer group relationships during this period are obviously an extremely important part of development. For some, the search for identity as an individual may proceed via an apparent submergence of individuality in a group identity. Particular kinds of music or dress code become important, and there may be intolerance of and even aggression towards outsiders. Much of this kind of adolescent activity is mainly still within the framework of ordinary family life (Hunter and Youniss, 1982). However, in some circumstances, again particularly when young people have lost contact with their families or communities, the identity and sense of belonging offered by the group may be a powerful pull towards antisocial or self-destructive behaviour. Young drug addicts on the streets of London, for example, develop their own language, their own moral code and their own sense of shared destiny. Encouraging young people to come off drugs means asking them to give up this network of familiar people and places and to try to create for themselves a very different way of life and identity.

Issues of power and control

As the Gillick ruling suggested, 'wise' parents gradually relinquish the right to control their children's lives as they move through the teenage years. Where this negotiation about areas of responsibility and choice take place within a secure, caring relationship, it is likely that tensions can be resolved. Where there is a history of abuse or neglect, it is likely that young people will find it hard to trust adults. Often a cycle develops in which the more the adult tries to control the child, the more the child needs to assert herself in opposition. This can occur in intact families or in substitute care. Teenagers can be overwhelmed with anxiety, both at the prospect of a complete lack of boundaries and at the prospect of an excessive use of power by adults.

Internalising and externalising behaviours

Although the evidence is that only a small minority of adolescents experience severe disturbance, it is often this group who will cause concern to social workers. Where there are problems in negotiating the tasks of adolescence, it may be helpful to think about responses to stress in terms of *internalising* and *externalising* behaviours. Although these are not entirely discrete categories, they help with understanding the psychological mechanisms involved.

One of the most worrying internalising disorders in adolescence is depression, which appears to increase significantly in the teenage years, particularly between the ages of 15 and 19. Depression is a flatness of affect associated with a sense of powerlessness or helplessness and a loss of interest in life rather than with obvious unhappiness. Rutter and Rutter (1993) suggest that depressive disorders in adolescence involve:

- negative thoughts about the world and the future (self-blame, worthlessness and hopelessness)
- social impairment (reduced capacity to work and enjoy leisure)

● somatic symptoms (insomnia, loss of appetite and psychomotor
  retardation or agitation).

Depression is a common feature of suicide, and rates of suicide and
attempted suicide rise during the teenage years, again especially
between 15 and 19 years. Suicide rates are considerably higher among
adolescent boys than girls, whereas *attempted* suicide rates are considerably higher among girls. Attempted suicide should always be taken
seriously, not only as an indication of emotional distress, but also
because many who do commit suicide have made previous attempts.

Emotional difficulties in adolescence are commonly associated with
problems at school. Under-achievers suffer greatly in a system that
places emphasis on academic success. Children who have experienced
physical or emotional deprivation are more likely to under-achieve
and to feel increasingly rejected and marginalised at school. Children
in foster or residential care already feel 'different', and moves of school
combined with under-achievement can lead to serious emotional and
behavioural difficulties.

The most recent concern in relation to internalising behaviours
relates to the increase of eating disorders, of which girls are at far
greater risk than boys. As with other aspects of development, there
appears to be a complex mix of social and psychological causal factors
here, with body image and the social valuing of thinness being significant (Attie and Brooks-Gunn 1989). Cases involving eating disorders
have raised serious dilemmas for social workers, doctors and the courts
as judgements have had to be made on whether a teenage girl whose
weight has fallen dangerously low can or should be forced to accept
treatment against her will.

Conduct disorders and antisocial acts can be described as *externalising* behaviour. Minor acts of delinquency are extremely common,
and for most teenagers this is a transitory phase. Young people who
exhibit more persistent antisocial behaviour and delinquency may be
part of peer groups in which this behaviour is the cultural norm, or
they may be unsocialised loners who have more complex psychological
problems. As with drug and alcohol use, minor delinquent acts are
now so common among young people that social workers need to look
closely at the psychosocial context to determine the seriousness of such
behaviours in a young person's life. They also need to get close enough
to the young person to establish the *meaning* of the behaviour to the
young person.

Age and understanding

- Adolescence is a time of transition but not necessarily a time of conflict. The establishment of an adult identity and the increasing capacity to make life decisions makes this a time of flux and change.

- Peer groups have a very powerful influence, but family ties remain very important for most young people. Adolescents have a continuing need for attachment relationships. For some chaotic adolescents who have few resources and may have been rejected by their families and excluded from school, the social worker should be aware of the need for a secure base. In some cases, it may need to be the social worker herself who provides this by being reliable and consistently concerned for the young person.

- At the point at which young people leave home, they will continue to rely on family figures. Teenagers looked after by the local authority will need additional help, both in establishing themselves practically and, more importantly, in having a secure emotional base. Young people who have experienced adversity, particularly abuse or neglect, and have low self-esteem may find the changing nature of family and peer group relationships very stressful. They may react with internalising or externalising behaviours or both. Understanding the developmental processes and the psychosocial context is essential.

- Developmentally, it is appropriate that teenagers are able to take more responsibility for the decisions that affect their lives. However, most teenagers continue to need the chance for consultation with adults who are trusted by the young person and can treat the young person with respect and support them in expressing their wishes and feelings.

Further reading

Bee, H. (1997) *The Developing Child* (New York: Longman).
This is a core student text summarising research on child development in a way which is very accessible to social workers. Although it is an American book, it includes international research. It also raises 'real world' issues such as teenage parenting, and is regularly updated.

Dunn, J. (1988) *The Beginnings of Social Understanding* (Oxford: Blackwell).

Dunn, J. (1993) *Young Children's Close Relationships: Beyond Attachment* (Newbury Park, CA: Sage).

Judy Dunn's research on the normal development of young children gives an important context for understanding children who have developmental problems. She also offers a model that draws on theories other than attachment theory.

Howe, D. (1995) *Attachment Theory for Social Work Practice* (Basingstoke: Macmillan).

Howe's book provides an excellent account of attachment theory, both Bowlby's original formulation and as it has since been developed theoretically and through research. Attachment continues to be a key theory for social work with families, and this text is essential reading.

Rutter, M. and Rutter, M. (1993) *Developing Minds: Challenge and Continuity Across the Life Span* (Harmondsworth: Penguin).

Rutter and Rutter describe development across the life span in a way which puts aspects of child development in context. Michael Rutter has been an immensely influential writer in the field of developmental psychology, and this book provides a useful summary of the research from a British perspective.

PART TWO

Working with Children in Practice

3

The Voice of the Child in Practice

Introduction

The focus of this chapter is working with children. We have resisted calling this 'direct work' or 'therapy' because the ability to work competently and sensitively with children should be a basic skill in child and family social work rather than a specialist activity. The child's right to a voice, as we have argued, pervades all social work with children and young people as well as featuring in several areas of the Children Act 1989 (see Chapter 1). This is not to say that some children will not need more intensive play therapy or specially planned long-term individual work. The aim of this chapter, however, is to enable workers to make a confident start in working and communicating with children of all ages. These beginnings can be developed into more creative, imaginative and longer-term work.

Work with children involves the use of play, conversation and observation to get to know and understand the child. Much of the work will be in ascertaining children's wishes and feelings, for a variety of different purposes. These can include:

- advocating on behalf of children when decisions need to be made that will affect them
- helping the child to participate in decisions in person
- preparing the child to attend meetings or court
- helping children to voice their opinion to a family member
- aiding children and young people to live through periods of crisis or uncertainty
- helping children deal with feelings of loss and bereavement.

Methods of work

Work with children involves varying degrees of intensity and a range of methods that should be chosen and adapted to suit the needs of the child in the particular situation in which she finds herself.

Play therapy methods

Some of the work can borrow from the aims, values and techniques used in play therapy (see Wilson *et al.* 1992). Play, rather than talking, is used as the major means of communication. Play can be seen as the means whereby the child manages the transition between the inner world of unconscious processes and the outer reality of home, family or school. The therapist can interpret the unconscious material presented by the child's play but also direct the play by using particular games or techniques. Links are made between the child's overt behaviour and her hidden unconscious feelings.

Some play therapy is structured, a variety of techniques being offered to guide the child into areas of play that will enable the child and therapist to explore problems or difficulties, using for example the ideas of Gestalt writers such as Oaklander (1978). Non-directive play therapy is less structured. It allows the child freedom to choose play material and will follow the child's lead. Non-directive play therapy has its roots in Rogerian client-centred therapy with adults. All of this work, whether directive or non-directive, is carried out within a special relationship between the child and the therapist:

> where the therapist creates a safe and trusting climate in which the individual is free, if he chooses to do so, to express and explore some of his feelings. (Wilson *et al.* 1992:1)

It is the therapist's role to listen and respond to the feelings that the child expresses through play. Many of the benefits the child derives from such therapies can also be achieved in a less ambitious but equally important way from sensitive, well-planned work with a social worker. Whether it is concerned with therapeutic play activities or helping the child with practical arrangements as well as emotional turmoil, children can come to experience security and reliability from within this relationship. For many children, their overpowering or overwhelming feelings can be contained by the worker who is listening, understanding and responding. By helping the child to communicate feelings, the worker can begin to help the child to achieve some control over them so that 'his life begins to have more coherence, pattern and meaning' (Berry 1978, in Wilson *et al.* 1992:1).

CASE STUDY

Play therapy

Alex is aged 8 and has been in foster care since he was 2. He has been diagnosed with attention deficit and hyperactivity disorder and is in mainstream school. His school career has, however, been punctuated by periods of suspension because his behaviour is difficult for the staff to manage. Like many children with this disorder, Alex has no friends and seems to be bullied at school. Helping Alex to express his feelings faces the worker with particular challenges since Alex does not seem to understand the language of feelings, and establishing a relationship is not easy. Helping children to recognise and name feelings is at the core of play therapy work, and many children need help to rediscover their senses through tactile materials like clay, water and sand. However, Alex does not respond to these methods of play, so they must be adapted. Sessions with Alex work best little and often – 10 minutes seems to be the optimum time to keep him engaged. The sessions are carried out at a room in school. Each question to him is prefaced by his name – 'Alex, tell me…' – and eye contact is needed at the same time. Work on feelings becomes more possible through the use of a school computer, with which Alex feels very comfortable. The computer helps Alex to communicate more easily and has helped to extend the sessions to 15 minutes. Alex is gradually able to express more about his life at school and to describe occasions when he is bullied. Wishes and feelings are not described in the same way as with most other 8-year-olds, but Alex does allow a worker some access to his own world. Progress with Alex seems slow and limited, but the work is extremely important in giving him a voice and protecting his interests at school and at home.

Methods of negotiation

Work with older children and adolescents in particular can involve mediation skills. The Department of Health publication *Focus on Teenagers* (1996b) calls for greater emphasis on direct work with teenagers and families. It highlights in particular that young people who have been 'in care' will often need a 'champion' to work alongside them, particularly when there is discord between the adolescent and her family. Mediation skills and conflict resolution are singled out as methods that are frequently very effective in bringing about some degree of rapprochement between families. Young people in care, or about to leave care, often want to renegotiate family relationships and need help in order to do this successfully. Young people living at home with problems that spill over into their life at school can also benefit from mediation and negotiation.

CASE STUDY

Negotiation
Richard is 14. His parents are seeking a divorce and there is considerable acrimony between them. Richard's school work has deteriorated; he has been getting into fights at school and was recently suspended for a few days. Two weeks ago he assaulted his father after hearing a bitter argument between his parents. He is now refusing to see his father.

Negotiation with Richard in these circumstances could come in a number of guises. The social worker could negotiate with Richard himself or act as a mediator for Richard with his parents, and with Richard and the school. The social worker, when acting as a mediator, should have no stake in the dispute and have no power to impose a settlement on the participants, each of whom retains the right to make his or her own decisions.

The aims and principles of negotiation remain the same whatever the forum for the negotiation:

● not to resolve disagreements but to help the individuals disagree
  in a more organised way
● not to resolve conflict but to manage it
● not to make recommendations but to help the child and family
  decide, or agree to differ
● not to give advice but to provide information where needed.

Successful negotiation should result in all parties feeling satisfied that an appropriate deal has been struck. Controlled harnessing of the conflict could help to make communication between warring family members not just safer but actually possible. This would put Richard's contact with his father on to the agenda whereas, in the current circumstances, Richard sees contact as an act of disloyalty to his mother. What the process can aim to do is to help Richard learn to separate the problems that are his from the problems that belong to other family members (Mulhearn 1996).

A method of decision-making adapted from Maori practices in New Zealand called 'Family Group Conferences' fits within the category of negotiation. An independent co-ordinator with mediation skills is selected to plan the conference, prepare the participants and make the conference function. As in other methods of negotiation, the professionals control only the broad process rather than the outcome, which is determined by the family (including the child). The conference is a gathering of all family members, the concept of family being understood very broadly to include people who are particularly important to the child and will 'behave like family' on the day. The meeting has three distinct phases:

- information
- private family time
- recommendations.

The gatherings are usually held on family territory and are potentially much more child-friendly than the formal business-like meetings, which take place in offices and which children tend to find tedious and alienating. The conference itself may last for several hours, and the child can drift in and out of the meeting. The social worker's role is to act as a consultant to the family and to the child, and to report for the family or child as required.

Linking negotiation and loss

Loss features prominently in the lives of children who come into contact with social workers and is referred to in several chapters. Dealing with the child's sense of loss is one part of the work to be achieved; sensitive negotiations with parents and carers will always precede this work.

Negotiation and loss

Samuel is 9 and his brother Joseph 7. The family moved to the UK as refugees from Uganda 5 years ago. Their mother Patience has symptomatic AIDS and has approached social services for support in helping to plan for her children when she becomes seriously ill and in the event of her death. She does not want her children to know about her illness or the fact that she has an unknown but short period of time to live. Social services are able to offer foster care on a long-term basis should this be appropriate.

In this case, negotiation will need to be undertaken with adults on behalf of the children. Families have strong views about what children should and should not know, and these issues need negotiation and discussion with the adults before any work with the child can begin. A parent with AIDS, for example, may want her illness kept from her child, and a worker would need a very good reason indeed to breach this confidentiality. Information about family life is usually best passed on by family members when they choose to disclose it. Negotiation with the parent would not involve trying to persuade the parent of the advantages of allowing the children to be involved in planning their future and knowing about her illness, but providing information about the need to secure the best practical arrangements in the time frame available and the psychological benefits to children of being prepared for the death of a parent to help them grieve.

Once agreement has been reached with the parent about the extent to which the children can be involved in planning for the future, work includes acting as a link between the children and their family, and being a bridge in a practical and possibly also an emotional sense. Although the worker may be limited in the amount of family information he can divulge to the child, the social worker has an obligation to be clear with the child about his role in the child's life. The manner in which the information is conveyed needs careful thought, the end result being that children understand better what is happening and can ask questions to clarify confusions or indicate when they want to know more. What children are told should *inform* rather than confuse them.

An important part of the work with Samuel and Joseph, as with many children who come into contact with social services, will be helping them to make sense of complex and sometimes painful feelings and to come to terms with living with uncertainty. They will want to know:

- what is happening
- why it has happened
- what will happen next.

These questions need simple, careful and straightforward explanations. If Samuel and Joseph are allowed to become more aware of their mother's circumstances, they will need reassurance that they are not to blame for their mother's ill-health. They will need to be able to rehearse how much or how little to explain of their home situation to friends and at school. Children of the ages of Samuel and Joseph will also be preoccupied with concrete issues and may worry about:

- what will happen to their mother after she has died
- who will take care of them or meet their needs (for example paying their pocket money)
- how they (and other people) will cope and survive.

(Brown and Mitchels 1997)

In planning the future, these boys will also be helped if they can take part in the rituals surrounding their mother's death when it occurs and be offered the chance to attend the funeral and be included in the family's grief. These events can act as a last chance to say goodbye and help the children to know that the loss is real (Jewett 1994). Exercises to help children living with uncertainty and facing loss are included later in the chapter.

Key factors for working with children

The major factors to bear in mind in working with children and young people of all ages are the following.

Legal context

Understand the context of your practice as a social worker with children in general. A good starting point is the *Principles and Practice* Guidance (Department of Health 1989), which is a helpful summary of work with children and their families.

Agency context

Good supervision is essential to check that you are maintaining an objectivity about the child's whole situation and not imposing your own agenda onto the child's circumstances and selectively hearing what the child says. It should similarly ensure that personal resonances are recognised and support is offered in the most appropriate way. Supervision can help to ensure that you establish priorities within your workload in order to have the time to be able to develop a relationship with each child.

A place to work

It is not essential to have dedicated space to work with children. If your materials are carefully selected, they can be portable, and much work can be done in the child's own home. Negotiate with the child and her parents or carers about whether it would be better to use the child's own room or arrange to use the kitchen or a downstairs area that can be kept private for the period of time you will need. You will not be able to create the intensity of play therapy, but it will be easier to link the work with the child back in with the family. For longer-term work, the pattern can be varied so that you can negotiate to take the child out of the home.

Knowledge

Equip yourself with a good understanding of child development so that your expectations are appropriate to the child's stage of development and level of understanding. This will help you to tailor your work with the child to their individual and developmental needs.

In addition to knowledge about children in general, it is necessary to acquire knowledge about the individual child. The child needs to be understood in his or her own particular context. It is also important to reflect on what expressing a view might mean to this child, in the context of her family and circumstances, including religion, racial origin, and cultural and linguistic background.

Skills

Practical resources should be developed to enable the work to be carried out. These are likely to include a portable 'kit bag' of props

and materials for working with children of various ag
using these materials so that you can feel confident in offe
to the child.

Relationship

The ability to create a relationship is essential in developing the skills necessary to be attentive to the child. With this comes the willingness to respect the child and to see things from the child's point of view, be it through conversation, play or observation of the child's behaviour. In order to achieve this, accurate empathy, warmth and genuineness must be employed.

Honesty

In all stages of the work, it is important to be honest with children and provide them with information they can understand. Children in care have a scanty understanding of why they are not living at home (Morris and Wheatley 1995). Young people have only a vague notion of what it means to have their name on the child protection register (Shepherd 1994). Information-giving is a minimum requirement of partnership work, and children have a right to know what is happening when professionals intervene in their lives. When a 12-year-old boy in the study *Safeguarding Children with the Children Act 1989* was asked what advice he would give to social workers working with children, he said:

> They should confirm things with you, like my social worker does, they shouldn't just decide things without asking you what you think – they should confirm decisions with you so that you can say whether or not you agree with them. (Thoburn *et al.* 1996)

Genuineness, warmth and empathy

Most of the principles that apply to effective social work methods with adults apply also to work with children. The accurate empathy, warmth and genuineness found to be so effective by Truax and Carkhuff (1967) are also essential precursors for a helping relationship with children. Wilson *et al.* define accurate empathy as:

the ability to feel with those who are seeking help, and articulate these feelings, so that the client feels understood, and is helped in turn to a greater understanding of these feelings. (Wilson *et al.* 1992:22)

Workers may feel they risk taking on children's pain when they begin to stand in their shoes. This is a familiar reason for avoiding working with children, as Kroll says:

Working with children is painful. It is often about loss, anger, rejection, neglect and sadness; it is also often about limited options and second rate solutions. It touches private life in tender places, it is unbearable and makes us feel helpless, sad and angry. Many workers admit to keeping children at a distance in an attempt to avoid feeling these feelings, to protect themselves from the pain, and to preserve a sense of competence. (Kroll 1995:91)

Many children whom a social worker encounters will have emotional difficulties and severe dents in their self-esteem, but a child's day-to-day life is unlikely to be suffused with distress. Life at school may offer opportunities for fun; staying with grandparents at weekends can offer respite from violence at home; life at home or in care may have its ups as well as its downs. The child's life will contain smaller, more detailed pieces of varied experience than the major problem that may be presented to you. It is the worker's task to understand the small pieces of the child's life to get a sense of the larger whole and how the child is feeling and making sense of her world. Observing a child can help you to notice different aspects of the child's behaviour and emotional responses.

Accurate empathy requires the worker to see and understand the child as an individual within her own context and to attempt to gain access to the child's perspective. The professional's preoccupations may not be the same as the child's or those of the adults around the child. Do not presume to know how the child must feel in this particular situation – find out and learn from the child and from others who know the child well.

Warmth can be conveyed to the child through an approachable manner and an attitude of concern and caring. These are important if you are to offer yourself to the child as someone to play with, talk to or confide in. Over-effusive behaviour will not win over many children, and taking over is not your role since parents or carers will have day-to-day care and should not be undermined.

Children are adept at spotting *authenticity* and *genuine interest* and feel let down by adults who they feel do not have time for them. One 10-year-old girl from the *Safeguarding Children with the Children Act 1989* study (Thoburn *et al.* 1996) said:

> The judge called us in to ask us what we thought and then he didn't take any notice. I could tell he just wasn't listening.

Amy wasn't complaining that the judge had failed to act on her views (she was ambivalent about what she wanted); what she was concerned about was his apparent lack of interest in her as a person as well as her views.

A 14-year-old boy interviewed by Butler and Williamson (1994:187) also demonstrated the need for professionals to be genuine when he spoke of his experiences of being taken into care:

> All I ever got was a pat on the head. Nobody ever spoke to me about it – and I'm not one to go to somebody and talk about it. Professionals need to emphasise their willingness to listen and try to understand. If they're willing to listen, I'm willing to tell.

Both of these examples demonstrate that a genuine interest will help the child talk to the worker, who in turn needs to listen to the child and contain and anticipate the child's ambivalence.

Materials for working with children

The first task in working with children is to engage their attention. This will enable you to develop a relationship that will help you to learn from the child. The child will need to want to engage with you as a person. Conversation and a warm and open manner may not sustain the child's interest indefinitely and may well need bolstering with some props. You can get to know the child by playing with and talking about her own toys, or an adolescent's computer or collection of tapes. A modest collection of basic play materials that you bring with you can, however, help to provide variety and give you a sense of direction in the work. Even with direct methods of work, your materials should not be imposed on the child but used to negotiate with her how you will spend the time together. What you bring with you can also explain who you are and what your role is, in the same way that the child's own surroundings tells you things about her.

Techniques and resources should be adapted for each individual child from within a basic 'kit bag' of play materials and props. As well as toys and games, the kit should include a repertoire of different helping methods that can be adapted and fitted to the child's cognitive and intellectual ability, emotional maturity and individual situation. The 'kit bags' suggested are examples of materials that can be adapted and personalised. The main message is that the kit can be simple, portable, and easy for the worker to use with confidence to engage the child.

Pre-school-aged children

It is worth giving some thought to how to box and carry 'kit bag' items to make your play materials more versatile and attractive to the child. The animals, for example, could be kept in a small tin that can be a plaything in its own right. A small shoe box can act as a shed for the animals or a bed for the doll (with the cloth used as a cover). Children's shoe shops are usually happy to give away spare boxes, and differently sized boxes fitting into each other become a game in their own right. These materials can be varied and adapted by you and, importantly, by the child. These materials are all potentially interesting and probably familiar to babies as well as young children.

A BASIC KIT BAG (PRE-SCHOOL-AGED CHILDREN)

- play people
- animals
- small car
- small soft ball
- puppet or furry animal
- baby doll or similar
- piece of cloth (for example a scarf for playing peep-bo or imaginative games)
- very basic drawing materials (for example some A4-sized paper and a few washable felt-tip pens)
- play-dough or similar, kept in tubs

School-aged children

For school-aged children, many of the materials for younger children will still be appropriate, with some alternative items.

Again, the materials used with this age group should be ones with which you feel comfortable and familiar. Simple props such as stars or stickers can be used in a variety of ways, as described in the exercises below.

A BASIC KIT BAG (SCHOOL-AGED CHILDREN)

- furry toy or puppet
- simple book
- variety of drawing materials (different coloured paper, good choice of pens, pencils, rubber)
- stars and stickers and other collage material
- 'Post-it' stickers for messages
- modelling clay instead of, or in addition to, play-dough
- family figures
- cars, fire engines, ambulances

Adolescents

Adolescents are likely to be wary of gimmicks such as stars, but some like them, want in any case to be offered a choice of materials and may enjoy 'playing'. Others may be content just to talk, or to complete an ecomap or write or draw with you. The 'kit' for adolesecents is probably best contained within a folder that can be reserved for work with this young person with her own name on it. There is a vast range of attractive stationary available, and it is worth choosing simple items like coloured folders with care. New materials chosen with care convey to the child or young person a sense that she is valued. Shabby materials that have been used many times suggest a lack of concern in the young person as an individual. Once the worker knows the young person, it may be appropriate to assemble a more elaborate set of materials, but it is probably best to start in a low key manner with a minimum of props.

BASIC KIT BAG (ADOLESCENTS)

- folder to carry the materials
- simple but attractive drawing materials (pencil, crayons, and so on)
- choice of coloured paper and some collage items
- modelling clay (carried separately in a tub)

Activities about feelings

The materials in the kits for school-aged children and adolescents
need few additions to be used to carry out the following activities. The
star chart described below works well with children across a broad
spectrum of ages including many 4-year-olds and even the occasional
3-year-old.

Activity 1

MY STAR CHART

Materials needed:
- A4 paper
- stick-on stars, in a variety of sizes and colours if possible
- glue (if the stars are not already gummed)
- 'Post-it' labels

Explain to the child that you want to know who is in her family and who
are the important people in her life. Ask her whether she can tell you
this by creating a star picture. Ask the child to place him or herself in
the centre of the picture and arrange family members and other
important people around her – anywhere she likes. She can write on
the names of the people or tell you their names. The picture can be
built up to include friends, neighbours, teachers – even pets if these
are important to the child.

The finished chart may look like this, but each child will have her own way of positioning the stars. 'Post-its' can be chosen by the child instead of stars or to distinguish between different people.

(adapted from Borba and Borba 1982)

Creating this star picture is a simple way of helping the child to talk about life at home, at school or in other settings. It is also more interesting and colourful to compile than the better-known 'ecomap', (which may be a better choice for a similar exercise with adolescents). It provides an excellent basis for a discussion about the child's relation-ships. It can be used in conjunction with the 'worry bee' exercise (see below) to ask whether the child has anyone to confide in.

Activity 2

MY WORRY BEE

This activity gives children the opportunity to think about and express things that worry them through an activity rather than solely through language. It helps the worker to distinguish between the child's own concerns and those of parents or professionals.

Materials needed:

- a pre-prepared 'bee' body and wings as shown (without a face or stripes) cut out of yellow or orange card.
- A4-sized paper
- glue
- a black felt tip pen

Tell the child that this is a bee who takes care of children's worries – a worry bee. Explain that each of the bee's stripes could be one of the child's worries. Ask the child to choose a piece of paper and glue the bee's body on to the page. Ask the child to give the bee a face and some antennae (a happy face or a worried face, or a funny face – say, 'It's up to you'). While the child is doing this, or as she is finishing, ask her to think carefully about things that bother her or make her worry. What are they? The child can draw stripes on the bee and write the worries in the stripes. Alternatively, some children will prefer to tell you their worries and colour the stripes in plain black.

The completed bee might look something like this:

(adapted from Borba and Borba 1982)

This exercise was used in the *Safeguarding Children with the Children Act 1989* study (Thoburn *et al.* 1996) and worked well with children through a range of ages, including young teenagers. It offers the opportunity to check the child's own concerns with professional pre-occupations and the possibility to amend small problems to make the child feel better and listened to. For adolescents, the exercise may not work or may need to be adapted to be less childish. The South American concept of worry dolls (or people) could be used. These tiny people, traditionally made of colourful thread, 'look after' worries and can be kept under a pillow at night.

The worry bee exercise can be made more elaborate with velvet ribbon stripes for worries, pipe cleaners for antennae and white tissue paper wings, but it works extremely well in its simple form. Similarly, other insects can be used, such as ladybirds, spots being added to a cut-out ladybird to represent worries and so on.

Some children may tell you they have no worries and may be uncomfortable doing the exercise. Other children may say they have no worries but be happy to complete the exercise anyway. It is worth revisiting the exercise after a period of time. One 9-year-old girl made the worry bee in a calm but flat manner saying she had no worries. A year later, when she was living in different circumstances, the exercise was discussed and she said that things at that time were so bad she could not have talked about her worries, but now she felt much better and could talk about how things had been as well as her current worries.

The worry bee exercise can be adapted or continued by making a 'worry rock'. Children can decorate a special rock or stone, which can then be kept in a pocket and held when the child feels the need to in the way that 'worry beads' are often used in Mediterranean countries.

Activity 3

STONES IN THE BAG

This activity is designed to help children of all ages deal with death and is usually done in a group. It could work well with a family of siblings.

Materials needed :
- three stones (see below)
- cloth bag or pouch for each child

There are three stones. The first stone is a black rough stone which is semi-transparent when held up to the light. The second stone is dull and smooth and the third is a bright stone. The Apache Indian myth tells that when the tribe was overrun by the 'cowboys' they cried, and their tears spilt onto the rock and became caught in the rock. The worker gives the children the first stone and explains that this is sometimes what grief feels like, it is rough and black and you feel all your tears. The children are then given the second stone. They are then told that as you begin to get used to things, your journey in life gets a bit smoother, the edges round off, but it's still not always very bright. The third stone, it is explained, is for when life gets colourful and bright.

The children can take away the stones as a way of remembering the journey of grief and how it feels different at different times. They can also be offered when the worker leaves as a symbolic ending and a reminder of the work together.

(from Cronin 1997)

This activity can also be used to help individual children, including adolescents, deal with grief. The exercise could be used, for example, with a young mother relinquishing a child for adoption (see the case study of Sarah later in the chapter).

Activity 4

CREATIVE WRITING

A range of different writing techniques can help some children and adolescents express themselves

1. My journal

Creating a journal may be a way for adolescents to deal with loss. Ask the young person to record specific examples of what he misses and how he is feeling from day to day, charting any ups as well as downs. This provides a private way of recording experience that the young person might want to share or keep to himself.

2. Letter writing

This can be a way of dealing with unfinished business with someone who has died or someone with whom the child has lost touch. The letter can say to the person what the child never had the chance to say in person.

3. Unfinished sentences

Psychological tests, children's activity books and life story work often use the technique of unfinished sentences to help a child to express themselves. The sentences could be school based or friends based:

- School makes me feel . . . .
- Friends make me feel . . . .
- When I've got no-one to talk to at break time, I feel . . . .

or more general and open ended:

- I wish I could . . . .
- Sometimes I wonder . . . .
- I would not like to live without . . . .

Other sentences can be problem focused:

- I wish people would stop . . . .
- Sometimes I'm afraid to . . . .
- I feel like crying when . . . .

The exercise lends it well to different adaptations, and simple computer graphics make it easy for practitioners to design their own materials and customise them for the child they are seeing. Handwritten materials can also be extremely attractive. It should no longer be necesary or acceptable for workers to arrive to see a child with faded photocopies of material that has been handed round the office for years.

Activity 5

USING COMPUTERS

Children are accustomed to using computers at school, and many young people also have access to a computer at home. They are a useful medium for working with children of most ages, who can show off their prowess in front of a screen. Games can be played together and drawings created on many basic word processing systems. Specific packages can also be bought to help children express themselves and talk about feelings. 'Feelings Factory' (Being in School, Level 1, David Glasgow), for example, uses images, sound and speech to help children to talk about their experience of being in school and their relationships with other children. The use of graphics means that all children, including those with communication difficulties, can choose pictures to represent themselves, peers and adults in school settings and use 'feelings faces' to describe being with these people. The package is designed to help children talk about difficulties in peer relationships, bullying and academic problems.

Children using packages like this do not need sophisticated language or literary skills so the packages are potentially extremely versatile. It may become clear, however, in the course of using a programme, that some children have trouble in understanding and naming feelings even in this straightforward way. This discoverery can help to establish therapeutic work that will need to be carried out.

The process

It is important to bear in mind that the work will happen in different stages, each with different concerns. Planning for the work should bear in mind when the work is likely to be concluded or reduction of contact, signalling a change in the nature of your relationship with the child. You should also anticipate a middle point. Not all energies should be focused on the early encounters, although getting these right and establishing a good relationship through early rapport is crucial.

Beginnings: making the best preparations; starting the work
The work

Before starting out, you need to consider:

- What is the purpose of your work?
- How long is the work likely to continue (for example, is there a time limited number of sessions)?
- What is the nature of your relationship with the child?
- What methods will you use?
- What materials/equipment?
- How will you record the work for the child, the family, the file, for supervision?

The child in context

It is essential to seek out background details to make sense of the child him or herself and the child's family background and current circumstances:

- What background information do you need about the child?
- How will you pitch your work to the child's developmental level/interests?
- What are the advantages for the child of doing the work with you?
- Are there any disadvantages?

Middle stages: doing the work; evaluating progress

You need to keep thinking about:

- What sense is the child making of the work with you?
- Are your methods effective? Do they need to be altered?
- How is the work with the child affecting siblings, parents and other family members?
- Is your communication with parents or carers and other members of the family effective?

Endings: concluding the work; ending the relationship

Well before you say goodbye, you need to consider the following:

- Have you achieved your shared aims?
- Will your relationship with the child finish or alter?
- How will you mark the end, or the changing nature of your work with the child?
- Does the child have someone else to confide in?
- Will the child be able to get in touch with you or another social worker if she needs to?
- Will the child have the confidence or ability to seek help, or can someone act on her behalf?

The process of working with children will be examined using case studies of children of different ages from varying ethnic backgrounds and in different circumstances. The case studies of such children described below demonstrate the variety of contexts and situations in which a social worker can be involved with the child. Some of the work involves brief short-term interventions; other involvements will be over longer periods, sometimes years. Some of the cases show how, at an early stage, it is difficult to predict how long the family will need support or how long you will be working with the child.

CASE STUDY

The pre-verbal child

Leon is 10 months old and has had two major moves in his life. He moved to live with his grandmother when his mother, a single parent, went to prison when he was 8 weeks old. He then moved to live with another member of the family when his grandmother had trouble coping. Leon was 6 months old by this time. His mother is due to be released from prison in 6 weeks. There were serious concerns about her ability to provide adequate care for Leon before her imprisonment. Work will need to be done with Leon to prepare him for a return to his mother.

Getting things right

Consent

Before you start to talk or play with a child, you will need to gain consent from parents or those with parental responsibility. This then needs to be communicated back to the child, who knows he has permission to be with you. Young children in particular, and babies like Leon, need to see as well as hear that their carers are allowing you to be with them. Parents or carers also need to see that the child is comfortable with you in order to have faith in your competence.

Explaining your role to the child

For babies and very young children, encourage the parent or carer to introduce you simply, with your help as needed. The younger the child, the less likely it is that you will be seeing him alone without his primary caretaker. With babies, a large part of the work with the child is observation of the child and of relationships with others around him. Language is nevertheless very important, and babies need to have newcomers introduced to them and need to be spoken to directly.

Listening to very young children requires heightened observational skills. The fine detail of how Leon behaves and how he exhibits pleasure, curiosity, anger, stress or anxiety needs to be studied. The child has a 'voice' from birth onwards that those well attuned to the child will understand.

Play offers the perfect medium through which a child's development and security or insecurity can be observed and through which you can develop a relationship. Leon could be offered your toys, and you could encourage him to play with you. Bringing the same toys each time could help Leon to remember you and consolidate his link with you. Interpreting play needs considerable care, and parents, nursery workers or others may be well placed to help the social worker to put the play in its context for the child. Pugh and Rouse Selleck (1996) explain that many young children cope with stress through play:

> Rich fantasy play needs to be taken seriously instead of dismissing weapons and noisy activities as bad behaviour or problems... Observations of patterns in play can help parents and professionals to listen to children thinking and learning. (Pugh and Rouse-Selleck 1996:11)

CASE STUDY

The verbal pre-school child

Parveen is 4 years old and the oldest of four siblings. Her family live in a two-bedroomed maisonette in an inner city. The family came to the area from a rural community in India 4 years ago. Parveen speaks

Bangladeshi at home and understands some English. Social services became concerned about this family because of reports from neighbours about fighting and violence between the parents, and because Parveen was seen cutting her 3-year-old sister with a knife while playing outside.

Religion, 'race' and culture

Before considering work with any child, it is necessary to think about the implications of 'race', religion and culture for the child and her family. These issues become more self-evidently relevant for members of minority ethnic groups, where English is not their first language and no mutual understanding can be assumed. At an early stage, it is important to gauge the family's attitude to your working with the child and their views about the child's right to be seen as an individual.

Groups emphasising collective good and collective responsibility may feel that seeking the individual view of the child and giving this prominence undermines cultural beliefs. The family may have strong opinions about whether their child should be offered a say, and this may be linked to particular religious or cultural attitudes about the role and place of children. If a family thinks that the child's views should not be represented separately from the parents' opinions, the work will have to be planned very carefully. The differences your involvement might make to the child's relationship with the family if your intervention risks transgressing these beliefs is an important consideration.

Parveen, at the age of 4, will not be involved in making significant decisions, and the issue is more pronounced for older children. The principle of her having a right to a say still exists, however, even at the age of 4. It will be essential to talk with Parveen's family to explain why you want to work with Parveen and what you will be doing together. In this way, you can begin to establish the family's attitudes to children being consulted in their own right, and you can negotiate permission to do the work with the child. These steps are important for all families and not only minority ethnic groups or religions. Parents and carers need information and support to reassure them that their parental role with the child is not being undermined.

If, as with Parveen's family, English is not the first language, ensuring understanding on all sides becomes more crucial, and it is important to consider using an interpreter who is acceptable to the child and family. The child's use of English may be better than her parents'. In these circumstances, the child should not be used to interpret between you and the family. If the child acts as interpreter, she is put in an invidious position. She may find out more than the family would wish or may misunderstand and become confused, only partially understanding what is happening.

Working with young children in this age group and ascertaining wishes and feelings will still require examining the way in which the child relates to important people around her. Attachment theory can make sense of these observations and provides helpful explanations for behaviour and relationships. For Parveen, however, the eye contact that can indicate attachment may be absent because eye contact is not encouraged by this or many Asian families as it is seen as a sign of disrespect.

Explaining your role to the child

Enlisting the help of parents and carers to explain who you are is useful for children of all ages but, from around the ages of 2 or 3, you can offer more direct explanation to the child herself.

EXERCISE   **ME AND MY ROLE**

Compile a small album of photographs to show to the child to put you in your professional context. These can depict you at your work base, in your car, in a meeting, seeing parents and playing with other children in their homes or in different settings. These images can help a child to make sense of what you do and where you come from. If you are going to be returning several times to see the child, it is helpful to leave a memento, for example a photocopy of your photograph, to help her remember you and to give you a context.

The child would probably be sitting on a parent's lap or near to a parent so these explanations also provide an indication to parents of what you do. Any material left with a young child will need to be in the safekeeping of a parent or carer, who will also need to understand its

---

purpose. With Parveen's family, it would be helpful to go through these explanations with an interpreter to avoid misunderstandings. It highlights the importance of a good explanation of your role to Parveen's parents. Working with a family where English is a second language reinforces the need for clear simple information for children and families.

Working with school-aged children

As children reach school age, they begin to make the shift towards more highly developed mental processes and become better able to focus attention. However, the 5-year-old who is fluent in language and can tell a good joke still has difficulty in seeing things from different perspectives. Things tend to be all good or all bad; friends are loved or hated. Susan Harter's work on children's self-esteem has shown that some time between the age of 5 and 7, children are likely to start making judgements about themselves that are more differentiated. When this happens, they can see themselves as, for example, good at some things but not others.

In terms of working with the child, mixing play with some simple questions becomes possible. However, Garbarino and Stott provide a note of caution:

> The basic approach is to take nothing for granted, to rely on modes of communication familiar to the child, and to constantly be on the alert to the possibility of misunderstanding in both directions. (Garbarino and Stott 1992:179)

Concrete thinking is a powerful force for all children in this age range. In the early stages of research in the *Safeguarding Children with the Children Act 1989* study (Thoburn *et al.* 1996), we made the mistake of asking children whom they were 'close to' in the family. Problems were soon apparent when we realised that one 10-year-old was interpreting this as the person sitting nearest to him. Use of language needs to be given careful thought and kept simple. Children of all ages, particularly young school children, are also very sensitive to what they perceive as adult expectations and are likely to tell a social worker what they think he or she wants to hear.

School-aged child
Alison is 11 and has two younger half-brothers. Her mother, a single parent, has mild learning disabilities and arthritis. From time to time, she requests accommodation for the children or asks neighbours to care for them. Alison feels responsible for her younger brothers when they are away from home and for her mother when they are at home. Alison was recently sexually assaulted by an acquaintance of her mother. Alison is going to be giving evidence in court against the person whom she says assaulted her.

'Age', from the welfare checklist, can also be interpreted as developmental level. What can be expected of children at different ages and stages and their 'evolving maturity' will obviously be affected by their individual experiences. At home, 11-year-old Alison appears mature and responsible in caring for her siblings; at school, she is difficult and demanding of the teacher, a bully in the playground but also a frequent victim of bullies. The overall apparent maturity of an 11-year-old like Alison who has also experienced sexual abuse will be different from that of a similar child without this background.

Many children who come to the attention of social services because they are in need, or are suffering or likely to suffer significant harm, may, like Alison, take on responsibilities for their carers or siblings and appear precociously mature. The cognitive and emotional maturity may not match their apparent coping abilities. It is important to pitch the work at the right level so that the child will understand what is being asked and benefit from her time with you. Make sure you are aware of the cognitive abilities of the average child of this age. Do not exceed these in your expectations of this particular child.

Alison is likely to need social work support for at least a year. The work will need to cover different phases and different aspects of Alison's life. First, there are issues relating to court: the uncertain and lengthy period in the build-up to giving evidence, dealing with the stress of giving evidence in court, and the aftermath, when Alison's abuser may or may not be convicted of the offence. Although guidance relating to evidence-giving means that Alison cannot be given therapy while she waits for court, she can be offered help and emotional support. Close liaison will be necessary with a legal department to ensure that work will not jeopardise the court case, but this does not preclude the use of play-based activities. Most importantly, however, the worker will need to be a consistent and reliable figure who can act as a source of information and reassurance. A social worker fulfilling a supportive and continuing role with Alison will take some of the strain from Alison's mother, and this will in itself be therapeutic for the child.

The second role in the work with Alison will be in monitoring and supporting day-to-day life in the family. In the year ahead, Alison's mother will need help in caring for Alison and her siblings, and planned respite or accommodation will be better than waiting for crises to occur. Alison can play an active role in negotiating this with the worker but will need to be protected from shouldering the responsibility for her mother and siblings.

A third element in the work with Alison will be liaison work on behalf of Alison with the school where she is having difficulties. Security needs to be fostered in the classroom and in the playground so the bullying stops. School-based staff need to be kept aware and helped to understand when there are changed circumstances at home and if Alison has periods living away from home. They also need to be made aware of when she will be going to court.

There are good opportunities in a case like this to plan the work, to provide consistency and to gauge how the work and the relationship with the child is developing. Empathy, warmth and genuineness will be the guiding principles, and elements of negotiation can also be used with Alison. Play therapy may be an important element after the court case has been heard. The work will vary in its intensity over the period of time, and the worker will need to be sensitive to Alison's changing needs, above all being consistent and reliable. When the work is completed or the case transferred, the end will need to be marked and well planned.

Children aged 12 and above

Adolescents also need a careful explanation of your role and involvement with them. The following exercise provides a format for information-giving, which can be offered to the young person at first meeting or in the early stages of the work.

EXERCISE   **INFORMATION SHEET**

Construct an A4-sized sheet explaining how you can be contacted, including a paragraph or so outlining aspects of your job, your connections with other professionals and the extent of your role as an advocate for the child. Explain the extent to which your work with the child is confidential, but if you use the word 'confidential', explain what it means. Everything should be in clear simple language.

You can, to an extent, use this sheet to advertise yourself and the services you offer. Adolescents are no different from adults in their sense of confusion about a social worker's role. The efforts you make to clarify your role for yourself, with each child and with each child's family can only be helpful.

The same sheet might work for several different young people, but check in advance whether or not the sheet needs to be adapted to the circumstances of each child. A basic sheet to work from and adapt makes translating into other languages, including Braille, or converting written material into an audiotape possible. Word processors make adaptation an easy task and provide simple ways of transforming what could be a dull business-like letter into something visually attractive. With a pre-prepared sheet to leave behind for the young person to check details alone or with parents or carers, you can gauge how much detail you need to go into with him or her on your first contact. Do not presume, however, that the young person is able to read what you have written or will indeed want to read this sheet.

CASE STUDY

Older children

Sarah, at the age of 17, has little sense of stable family life. She has not lived with her birth family since the age of 2 and has experienced a number of different foster home breakdowns. She has mild learning disabilities and asthma. She became pregnant when she was 16 and was persuaded to offer the baby for adoption, no longer having contact with her son. Since her pregnancy, Sarah has regained some limited contact with her mother after an estrangement of many years. Her mother can offer her limited but important support.

From 12 or so onwards, children are moving away from concrete thinking to acquiring more sophisticated cognitive skills – in Piaget's terms, 'formal operations'. For some children, this is not achieved until 15 or later, and for some others not at all. Young people who are at this level should be able to think about the possible as well as the actual, and can think and make choices about the future. Contributing feelings and opinions for children who have reached this stage is developmentally possible, but emotional maturity may not coincide with cognitive ability.

The degree to which a young person should be responsible for major decisions will depend very much on individual circumstances. Many older children, particularly in divorce circumstances, do not want to be held responsible for letting down a parent by making a choice in favour of one rather than the other. In most cases, older children will want to exercise their opinions, even if the outcome is not perfect.

The child's special features and characteristics need to be considered at the planning stage and throughout the involvement. There is a need to discover the child's particular abilities or disabilities and losses as well as previous experiences of professional helpers. Children with learning disabilities or communication difficulties, like Sarah, may need extra help to be able to voice their views. Sarah, we are told, was 'persuaded' to give up her son, and we do not know the degree to which she had full involvement in this decision. She is likely to want to talk about this and needs the opportunity to talk through what her son's adoption means to her. It would be wrong for the worker to presume how Sarah is feeling – it is his or her responsibility to find out from Sarah herself, using the most appropriate methods. Sarah has experienced a number of losses and moves in her life, and a symbolic exercise such as the 'stones in the bag' may help her begin to understand her feelings about events in her life, in particular the loss of her baby.

The long-term aims of working with children to ascertain their wishes and feelings should be for the child to develop the capacity to exercise choice and have informed views as a maturing young person and as an adult citizen. The child needs to practise these skills within the family, and work undertaken with the child should reinforce rather than undermine this possibility. If the child is not with the birth family but in a foster home or a residential setting, as Sarah is, there are two 'families' to be borne in mind, and the child's links with the current carers and with his origins should be remembered.

Conclusion

There are constant themes that need to be borne in mind when working with children. It is important to help children of all ages to exercise increasing choice and ultimately control over their lives as they mature. There is a responsibility on all workers to ensure that the child has a degree of control and choice in the work done with you and consents actively to answering questions, playing games or choosing where the play work is to take place. Remember that, until most children are 10 or 11 years old, they may not be able to say that they do not know, cannot remember or do not fully understand.

Monitoring and assessing the child's ability and receptivity to the work you are doing is an important element of the work. Be alert to the child's interest and enthusiasm; watch the child's body language for signs of stress. Intersperse drawing with talking, let the child choose a new activity and choose when to rely on conversation.

Your preoccupations may be different from those of the child so avoid a mindset about what you think is of major concern to the child. Attempt to establish whether the child's views change from day to day or whether you are being told what the child wants you to hear. Understand the child's concerns from their whole context – their life at school or with grandparents, as well as at home and problems with friends as well as with relatives.

Some aspects of the child's wishes should be followed through. Because the child may not be allowed, or may not want, the final say in major decisions, it is essential that some aspects of the child's views be acted on. Tackling some worries, such as bullying at school, may make living with largely irresolvable family problems easier to cope with. Exercises like the 'worry bee' may help in identifying the child's concerns. Helping even very young children to have a say in day-to-day matters will enable them to see that their opinions are important. This should improve the quality of their life.

Further reading

Department of Health (1989) *The Care of Children: Principles and Practice in Regulations and Guidance* (London: HMSO).
This is an essential text for child care practitioners and provides a good foundation for work with children.

Department of Health (1996) *Focus on Teenagers: Research into Practice* (London: HMSO).
This is a summary of three research studies on adolescents which analyses the findings and draws implications for practice. It contains a helpful section entitled 'Tools, checklists and exercises'.

Garbarino, J. and Stott, F. M. (1992) *What Children Can tell Us: Eliciting, Interpreting, and Evaluating Critical Information from Children* (San Francisco: Jossey-Bass).
A good guide to sensitive interviewing and pitching the work at the right developmental level for children.

Wilson, K., Kendrick, P. and Ryan, V. (1992) *Play Therapy: A Non-directive Approach for Children and Adolescents* (London: Baillière Tindall).
More detail about the theory and application of non-directive therapy.

4

Working with Children in Need and in Need of Protection

Introduction

Children first come to the attention of social services departments for a number of reasons. Some children may be living with parents who are not able to care for them adequately. These shortcomings in parental care may be temporary or of long standing. They are likely to stem from a multitude of factors and may, in some circumstances, amount to neglect or maltreatment of the child. Many children from these families and others have problems in their own right. Some children are disabled; others have emotional and behavioural problems and, as such, may become beyond the control of parents at home and teachers at school. It is often at times of distress or crisis that help is needed for children within their families. That help can come in the form of voluntary support and services or statutory enquiries to check on the child's safety and well-being and provide protection. At this stage, work is primarily with children within their own families, although young people adrift from their own families can be offered services in their own right.

Maintaining children within their own families is seen by national and international law to offer children the best prospects for optimum development. The family can, however, be a source of pain, unhappiness and long-term harm for children who are maltreated or neglected. Cleaver and Freeman remind us that longitudinal studies, particularly in psychiatry, have shown that abuse in childhood poses risks to healthy development that is every bit as dangerous as serious childhood illness (Cleaver and Freeman 1995:5). Although the family can be a source of danger to the child, supporting the family will, in most cases, be the best way to protect the child. Hearn (1995) argues that the function of family support includes the need to protect children and provides a constructive context for protection to occur.

Yet, in spite of the official rhetoric of 'family support', there is an ambivalence about the value of the family for all children. In recent years, some local authorities have effectively prioritised restricted resources so that only children in need of protection (from abusing parents) get a service. Other authorities have 'refocused' services with the aim of offering a broader base of family support to help sustain children in their families in ways more in sympathy with the spirit of both the UN Convention and the Children Act 1989.

The aim of this chapter, then, is to look at positive ways of working with children in need and in need of protection, both at the early stages when a service has been offered and when child protection enquiries have reached the stage of the interagency child protection conference. We recognise that there are many overlaps in these two areas of work, which have only recently been brought together. We examine the legal and policy framework for children in need and child protection and consider children's views of the process. We outline principles for good practice and illustrate how these might be applied in practice through case examples.

Legal and policy framework

Children in need

In order to qualify automatically for any support from the local authority under the Children Act 1989, we have already seen (Chapter 2) that a child must be deemed to be 'in need'. For this to happen, the child must be seen to need services:

- in order to achieve or maintain a reasonable standard of health or development (s.17(a))
- to avoid significant impairment of health or development (s.17(b))
- or because he or she is disabled (s.17(c)).

The definitions of need set out in s.17 form a gateway to all the services in Part III and Schedule 2 of the Act. These services range from advice and counselling (Schedule 2) to the provision of specific help such as accommodation and day care. Once a child has crossed the threshold and is considered to be in need, services can be offered to any member of the child's family and are not restricted to that one child. So, for example, the siblings of a disabled child can be offered any of the services and help listed in Part III and Schedule 2 as appropriate.

FAMILY SUPPORT SERVICES

- assistance in cash or kind (s.17(6))
- day care (s.18(1)(2); s.19(1))
- out-of-school care (s.18(5), (6))
- accommodation for adults, in order to protect child (Schedule 2, para 5)
- family centres (Schedule 2, para 9)
- advice, guidance and counselling (Schedule 2, para 8(b))
- occupational, social, cultural or recreational activities (Schedule 2, para 8(b))
- home help (Schedule 2, para 8(b))
- help with travelling to services (Schedule 2, para 8(b))
- holiday provision (Schedule 2, para 8(b))
- accommodation (including respite care) (s.20)
- publicity about these services (Schedule 2, para 1(2); and s.26(8))

One of the strengths of the new legislation is that this part of the Children Act brings disabled children into mainstream child care policy for the first time in almost a century (Baldwin and Carlisle 1996). An important minority of children living in England and Wales have disabilities and all are eligible for services. Schedule 2 of the Act makes clear that services for disabled children should be designed to minimise the effects of the disability and provide opportunities for living as normal a life as possible, thereby emphasising the importance of considering the ordinary needs of childhood. However, in practice, calculating the number of disabled children in the population is difficult because impairments can range from slight to very severe and definitions of disability tend to exclude, among others, children who are ill. Estimates quoted by recent OPCS surveys of disability have produced an estimate of 3 per cent of the child population, but the definition does not capture the full range of disabled children likely to need support (Baldwin and Carlisle 1996).

It is also clear that help and support under the Act are also being limited to children who are already perceived as being vulnerable or in need of protection (Children's Rights Development Unit 1994:3.4.4). Tunstill *et al.* (1996) found a number of identifiable groups of children at low priority for services. These were children with mental health needs, unaccompanied child refugees, children with significant emotional problems, children who were carers, children in transition to adulthood and children abusing alcohol and misusing substances. Whole communities are also sometimes found to be excluded from services, for example travellers, who are rarely offered services under s.17, even though their sites may be poorly equipped and hazardous places for children, offering real dangers to their health and development.

For an even larger group of children – the poor – it is unlikely that poverty will, of itself, convey entitlement to family support services, although being poor will almost always exacerbate any other difficulties that exist. Using the accepted European definition of poverty as those living on less than half the average income, 4.3 million children out of the total of 11 million children living in England and Wales were found to be in poverty in 1993 (Gulbenkian Foundation Commission 1995). Bebbington and Miles' influential article showed that children in families with low incomes and substandard conditions were many times more likely to enter care than were their counterparts living in average conditions (Bebbington and Miles 1989). The relationship between infant mortality, poor health and social class has become stronger as this gap between the rich and the poor has widened (Kumar 1993). Studies of nutrition have shown that poverty not only stunts children's growth, but also affects their ability to learn (Barclay 1995; Dowler and Calvert 1995). When material and social adversity is coupled with relationship difficulties, the effects on the child are more severe. Factors such as changing and inconsistent caregiving, family discord, quarrelling and hostility, and blame directed towards the child have been linked to psychiatric illness in childhood or adulthood (Rutter *et al.* 1990). Children living with parents overwhelmed by their own problems may need support or protection from outside the family. Gibbons *et al.* (1995)

demonstrated that parents of children who were considered by professionals to be vulnerable to abuse had profiles that included two of the following: substance abuse, a criminal record, psychiatric illness or violence to or from a partner. The same study and others have shown that little therapeutic help for the child or support for the family was offered once the 'investigation' phase of child protection work was completed:

> The care we are offering such children, most of whom have had no therapeutic post-protection work, seems to be sadly lacking. The process for them is painful and they are left feeling isolated and unhappy, wondering what has improved. The abuse had stopped, but so much else has been lost. (Trowell 1996:70)

Children in need of protection

Children thought to be suffering or likely to be suffering significant harm as a result of maltreatment or neglect from their parents may find themselves coming into the child protection system as a result of an enquiry under s.47 of the Children Act 1989. These enquiries enable the local authority to determine whether they need to take action to safeguard or promote the child's welfare. This includes considering emergency action to protect the child.

As a s.47 enquiry is pursued, the process of making enquiries and deciding whether or not to take action continues. The work is guided by the procedural document *Working Together* (Department of Health 1991c), which sets out these specific stages to be followed:

- pre-investigation
- first enquiry
- family visit
- the conference.

The child protection conference pools information from the professionals and family members present and determines whether the child is suffering or is likely to suffer significant harm, and whether there is a need for a multi-agency child protection plan. A decision is then made about whether the child's name should be included on the child protection register, which acts as a record of all children in the area in need of protection about whom there is an interagency protection plan. (Department of Health 1991c:41).

Out of approximately 160,000 annual child protection referrals, 23,000 will be unsubstantiated and will go no further than early enquiries (Dartington Social Research Unit 1995). Only a small number of child protection referrals prompt emergency protective action, so that, each year, only 1,500 children are removed, usually from home, under an emergency protection order. Many of these children will go back home but, as enquiries progress, others may move or be moved away from home. About a month after the first referral, and by the time a child protection conference has been held, only about 6,000 children (from the total of 160,000) will find themselves living away from home. Half of these will be accommodated and looked after by the local authority with their parents' and in some cases their own agreement; the other half will be away from home with the authority of the court (Dartington Social Research Unit 1995). By far the majority of children are still living at home or have returned home at the post-conference stage of child protection work.

Children as active participants

Being a child in need

The gateway to services is, as we have seen, to be a child in need. For most children, the notion of being 'in need' will be linked to mammoth fundraising events featuring bandaged teddy bears on the television; it will have nothing to do with seeing a social worker, receiving counselling or going to a family centre, foster parents or respite care. Getting a service or seeing a social worker is something that parents or family members tend to organise and children find out about later, often when decisions have already been made. Yet children can act to get help for themselves, as the 10 years'-worth of 30,000 calls a day to ChildLine have demonstrated (although we know that two-thirds of these calls do not get through to a counsellor). Even very young children aged 5 or 6 can be accustomed to summoning help for themselves or their parents, often via a public phone box (Epstein and Keep 1995; Brandon and Lewis 1996; Hill _et al._ 1996). Children with previous experiences of seeing a social worker or older children are aware that they can obtain services in their own right and can and do 'broker' their own access to help. Children tend to 'come back' when they have been received positively and have learnt to trust a worker.

Young people who are experiencing difficulties at home can ask to be accommodated by the local authority (under s.20 of the Children Act) even in the face of parental objections. Young people desperate not to return home may be suspicious of social services and choose to run away rather than risk a return to their family by asking for help from a duty social worker. Stein *et al.* (1994) identified abuse at home as a key factor in running away. Economic stresses on parents and resource constraints on local authorities were found to be important contextual factors in understanding the reasons why young people ran away.

Although help as a child in need is theoretically available to young people without first being filtered through their parents or family, help will not always materialise and young people are often turned away when they ask for asistance. Local policy may actively discourage duty social workers from offering services to children because of the shortage of resources, and this message is easily picked up by young people, who are reluctant to ask for help if they suspect that they will be turned away.

Being a child in need of protection

Children may know little of the child protection enquiries going on around them. We have already seen that a quarter of child protection referrals go no further than the first enquiry, and in these cases a child (and her parents) are unlikely to be aware that an enquiry is taking place. In other instances, children initiate action themselves: 'Me and my mum weren't getting on and it was my choice to contact the Social Services, I brought them into it, like' (Shepherd 1994:13).

However, even in these cases, as the enquiries progress children often feel unsure about what is happening. Shepherd, in her small study of 18 children over the age of 8 years involved in child protection procedures, points out that, although some children felt they were listened to, they were still no wiser about the next steps:

> they were not clear why information was being asked for and either they had forgotten why they were being interviewed or social workers had omitted to explain what the purpose of the investigation and assessment process was. (Shepherd 1994:14)

Once children know or suspect that their parents are being questioned about harming them, they may fear that their family will be split up or that they will end up in care. We have already seen that, in fact, only a small proportion of children are removed from home during this process, but the fear is acute and the reality very stressful.

Children will often feel confused and upset when they do have to leave home. One child said she was:

> Scared because I was going to a different family and I didn't know them, and angry because my Dad was abusing me and I had to move away from them instead of him. I didn't know what was happening. (NCH 1994)

Children may be reluctant to reveal the truth about abuse or maltreatment. Some children tell ChildLine that they withdrew their allegations of abuse against parents because they felt the system was rocketing out of their control; as one 14-year-old girl said:

> If you tell anyone about it it might get out of hand. They'll twist your story. It's better to sort it out your own way. (Butler and Williamson 1994:70)

Other children want enquiries to continue because they need the abuse they have suffered to be officially recognised. They want to be believed by adults and, most of all, they want the abuse to stop. However, not all children who try to tell adults about their experience of family life and abuse get heard. James' Social Services Inspectorate Report into 'Section 8' cases (cases of near death through maltreatment or neglect) highlights the fact that children in these cases were not listened to or taken seriously when they spoke of the harm they were suffering (James 1995). The moral rights that children have to be involved in decisions that affect their lives, and to express their wishes and feelings about their future, cannot be enforced (Schofield and Thoburn 1996). Some safeguards to participation exist in the child protection process, but they do not and cannot guarantee the ideal outcome that the child would most often want – the abuse to stop and the family to be kept together.

Within the debate of how to let articulate children participate, and under which system, it is possible for the needs of disabled children, for protection as well as support, to get lost. Some of these children we now know are even more likely to be maltreated or neglected by parents than are their non-disabled counterparts (Kelly 1992).

Principles underpinning work

Children on the threshold of services are likely to be living at home and experiencing a number of adversities and difficulties. Parents may be one of the sources of harm but, in most cases, families offer the best chances for the child's optimum development, and the work with the child will go alongside close links with the family.

The child's perspective on events is of crucial importance. It is also important to protect children from unnecessary stress and to:

> find a balance between enabling children to be involved whilst at the same time protecting them from exposure to stresses and conflicts inconsistent with their welfare. (Department of Health 1994:16)

The following principles for good practice include adaptations of guidance in *Working Together* (Department of Health 1991c) and *The Challenge of Partnership* (Department of Health 1994). They apply equally to work with children in need and with children in child protection, and build on the principles outlined in Chapter 3:

- *Keep the child in mind.* So-called child-centred practice is not always good at keeping the child in mind in all stages and phases of the work. When priorities are determined, assessments made and services offered or denied, professionals should keep uppermost in their minds how the child is feeling and is likely to be affected.

- *Try to make sense of the child's world.* Let other family members and professionals who know the child well help you to understand how this particular child feels, but also make sure to gain your own view from the child herself. Ensure that the whole context of the child informs the way you work with her and any decisions that are made (this will include religion, race and culture as well as the child's particular experiences). Look beyond the 'incident' in child protection work to ensure that the child's broader 'needs' do not get lost.

- *Work with the family.* Successful work with the child requires good involvement with the family. It is important not to undermine parents so that the work with child does not threaten her place in the family. Find out from the family as well as the child what services they feel they need or would like.

- *Give the child information.* Children need specially prepared information in a clear, interesting and understandable form about services and, where relevant, child protection procedures. This should be provided by agencies. Once a social worker becomes involved, the child needs to know specifically what is happening to her and and her family and why. It is important to check that the child *does* understand what has been communicated. Sensitivity is needed to know when to repeat or vary explanations and when this could amount to brow-beating the child. Children should be informed of the outcome of the relevant decision-making meetings.

- *Participation.* Opportunities should exist for children to participate in varying degrees according not only to their age and understanding, but also their own wishes. All children should be given a degree of control over what is happening and have their views heard and represented. Participation can take place *directly* through discussion and/or play with the social worker and through involvement in meetings or conferences; it can occur *indirectly* through what a child conveys of her feelings, often through behaviour, at home and in settings away from home (for example school or nursery) and via representation of her views by another person.

- *Consent.* Children of all ages should give informed consent to medical examinations and interviews (including videotaped interviews) and have a right to a say in the pace and extent of the enquiry or investigations and the work in general. With young children, ensuring consent is likely to require careful and sensitive observation of the child rather than direct questioning.

- *Confidentiality.* Confidentiality should be ensured to the furthest extent compatible with the child's best interests. Confidentiality should not be waived because this is a 'child' or this is a 'child protection matter'. A clear understanding about the meaning and limits of confidentiality should be part of the social worker's agreement with the child at the start of their work together.

- *Ascertaining wishes and feelings.* Finding out the child's perspective on events needs sensitivity. It is necessary to learn from children themselves what causes them distress and harm, and check this against the preoccupations of professionals and parents. For children who have been maltreated, ascertaining wishes and feelings needs to take into account the potential impact of emotional or psychological trauma. Betrayal of trust and hurt within the family is likely to prejudice the child's capacity to make sense of experiences. This is not an argument for not listening to children or reframing and qualifying what they say, but it is an argument for professionals to devote more time and develop greater skills in helping children think through their situation (Schofield and Thoburn 1996). Finally and most importantly, the child should gain a clear sense that there is respect for her and for her wishes.

What it is like for a child to be on the receiving end of support services needs to be given as much thought as does how children feel about being involved in enquiries about abuse. Important details need to be kept in mind – for example the impact on a pre-school child of travelling for 45 minutes on two buses twice a day to get to and from a funded nursery place. The strains on the mother are likely to be considered but less often so are those on the child who will bear the brunt both of the travel arrangements and of a parent's struggle to cope. For the child who comes into the child protection system, it is important that she be helped to recover from the harm or the difficulties at home. Workers should ensure that things are not made worse by the helping and assessment process the child initiates or finds herself caught up in. All these issues need to be borne in mind so that good professional practice is helpful to the child and so that she does not feel excluded.

Working with children in need

This section examines practice in the early stages for two children in need. We look in detail at a young person who asks for help in her own right and a pre-school child whose mother is seeking help in coping with her young son. The following section examines the work with two school-aged children in need of protection, exploring practice dilemmas and ways to involve each child in the process. The fine line between determining whether these children are in need or in need of protection is apparent in each case, and there are overlaps in all cases. The concern here, however, is the work with and on behalf of the child.

Asking for a service

Asking for a specific service might imply that the family or child already know what help they want, but this will still need further assessment. A request could be, for example, for day care or a paid playgroup place for a pre-school child, or a plea for regular respite or accommodation for a child of any age. By the time a child or family comes or is referred to social services, however, they are often desperate. The 'request' for accommodation may be a threat to leave the child at the office if help is not offered. Asking for a paid playgroup place could similarly come when the family is at the end of its tether. How the child feels about the family situation and the request for a service may not appear on the referral.

The problems in gaining access to services and determining which type of service a child needs (support or protection) have been made apparent. The picture becomes more complex when we consider the children's role in getting help for themselves. Some children act on their own initiative to get a service; others do not. The distinctions between those who act and those who do not are not linked simplistically to age. The first case example includes a young woman seeking help in her own right.

CASE STUDY

Melanie is just 16. She went to live with her father when he was released from prison for causing grievous bodily harm. This has not worked out for Melanie as her father drinks heavily and often does not come home. Melanie is very frightened of him. She cannot go back home to her mother, who has left the area and lives in sheltered housing because of a disability. Melanie wants to be accommodated by the local authority. In the past, she has had brief spells in foster care and residential care when relationships at home have broken down.

First contact

The possibilities for engaging the child and creating a trusting relationship (also with parents) may be coloured by earlier experiences of social services help or intervention. Families being 'assessed' for the first time provide workers with the opportunity to make good impressions and good relationships that can continue or be transferred if the child is to need long-term support. If the case is closed, a social worker who has listened and understood will make children feel that they can come back for help if it is needed.

Melanie and her family have been involved with social workers in the past and will already have previous experiences to build on. It is a positive sign that Melanie has felt sufficiently empowered to come and ask for help on her own. At the age of 16, Melanie will be closely involved in planning the services she needs if she is deemed eligible.

Further assessment

Melanie has hinted to the social worker that her father sexually abused her in the past. In recent weeks, she has spent much of her time living in a squat with young people whom she says are usually drunk or 'out of their heads'. Melanie is frightened here as well as at home with her father. Failure to respond to Melanie's request for accommodation could prompt her to run away from home. Her profile of a past in care and sexual abuse at home (in the past if not currently) would make her very vulnerable to homelessness and its ensuing problems (Stein *et al.* 1994).

The work with Melanie

Melanie's version of events has been checked and it is clear that neither parent can, nor wants to, care for her. Her vulnerability has been acknowledged and her request for accommodation accepted. Initial work with her will involve planning the services she needs, in particular finding the right placement. The social worker needs to develop a relationship of trust quickly with Melanie so that they can negotiate together and plan together.

Participation at meetings and conferences

Much of social work with children and their families at these early stages is carried out in the context of meetings that often involve a range of professional groups. Many children will be the subjects of these multi-agency conferences, either through child protection procedures or as children in need. Although these meetings are geared to adults' rather than children's needs, children are increasingly being invited to attend, sometimes without a clear view of the benefits they will derive from participating in person.

If Melanie is to play a full part in the decision-making process, she must show herself to be mature enough to attend meetings and keep to agreements with her worker. This is a tall order, and many adults in distress and needing social work help prove themselves unable to keep to agreements and to behave rationally all of the time (Howe and

Hinings 1995). It is unfair to expect more of teenagers, who are known to be volatile, than it would be reasonable to expect of an adult. Even though she is 16, Melanie may find meetings uncomfortable and may choose to have her views represented rather than present them in person. She may want to attend some meetings and not others. She should be helped, prepared and ecouraged to participate in person, but not browbeaten into attendance. If Melanie does not feel she gets on well with her social worker, a volunteer advocate could, in principle, be found for her; her views at meetings could also be represented in this way (Scutt 1995).

Establishing a relationship

Once the immediate arrangements have been clarified for Melanie, the social worker and Melanie will need to find a way to include Melanie's parents in decisions that are made about her in a manner that fosters good links and ensures that some level of contact can be maintained but does not undermine her safety. Keeping up contact with Melanie's mother who, until 6 months ago, was her main carer will be a priority. Gathering the family together and calling a family group conference would be a way to put the decisions and responsibility for Melanie's well-being back with the family. Melanie is very resistent to this idea and is very frightened about her father's likely reactions. She also feels that her mother has have never been a reliable support for her and that she cannot expect much from her family. Melanie is clearly looking for the 'champion' and 'mentor' that young people in accommodation need (Department of Health 1996b). There is considerable scope for a social worker (or residential worker or foster carer) to begin to develop this sort of relationship with Melanie from these early stages. Melanie needs a professional she can trust, who is not afraid to discuss sensitive topics and who is prepared to persevere in the face of the young person's minor transgressions (Department of Health 1996b:31). It is important not to rush precipitately into complex planning systems, such as a family group conference, which will at this stage alienate Melanie.

Working with the future in mind

This case could resolve itself relatively quickly if Melanie could be helped to rebuild the bridges with her family or find other supports. On the other hand, Melanie could be in accommodation long term and could need social work help through to her adulthood. Good beginnings with the social worker will ease this difficult transitional stage for Melanie.

The following case examines early work on behalf of a pre-school-aged child.

CASE STUDY

Steven is 2 and has a younger half-sister Bethany, who is 8 months old. His mother is a single parent living on income support. She has requested a paid playgroup place for Steven and says his behaviour is 'doing my head in'. The health visitor has confirmed that Steven is unusually aggressive and added the information that his mother is frequently depressed. Her responses to the children veer between ignoring them, shouting and swearing at them and being a capable and caring mother.

First contact

The first contact is likely to be in the office, when parents often bring toddlers and babies with them. Good practice dictates that the social worker or duty worker should use the first meeting with the parent to make early contact with any children of the family by talking with them and undertaking simple observation as a preliminary assessment. The observation could focus on three broad areas: the child's appearance and general demeanour, the relationship between the child and the parent, and the child's behaviour. In this case, some good early information has been provided by the health visitor, which can be added to; in other cases, the social worker would be the first person to make this early assessment of the child's overall well-being.

Observation

Early observation revealed that Steven was well nourished and well dressed. He was, however, pale with lack-lustre eyes and a somewhat anxious expression. When he went to his mother for comfort or reassurance, she rebuffed him. This was in stark contrast to her loving responses to the baby on her lap, who looked similarly well nourished but presented a much more contented demeanour. Steven would not settle to play with the worker or with any of the office toys and hurled the Lego around the room. His mother's reactions alternated between shouting at her son and ignoring him. It was easy to see that Steven's

at the end of her tether with him and that Steven's
nt was likely to be severely impaired in these circumstances,
)f significant harm (emotional and physical harm) being
ial. At this stage, Bethany appeared to be faring better in her
moth‿ ‿s care than her brother and at this stage seemed less 'at risk'.

Further assessment

This case has many complex elements and needs further assessment rather than merely providing what has been asked for. Without a good social work assessment, matching the needs with the most appropriate services will be haphazard. The task is not merely one of eligibility but is an assessment of the needs of the child and the family in a broader sense. More information is required to understand the child's world and his experiences.

More information reveals that Steven's behaviour is particularly difficult when Bethany's father, who has regular violent outbursts against his mother, has been visiting the home. Steven's development is possibly being impaired from the effects of witnessing domestic violence. Harm from domestic violence, unless the child is injured and 'caught in the crossfire', is regularly overlooked or minimised (Brandon and Lewis 1996) and has not been part of the professional mindset of how children might be harmed by their parents. Steven is likely to be a very frightened and confused little boy without the cognitive skill, at the age of 2, to make any sense of this recurring violence or his mother's inconsistent responses to him.

Without access to a social worker, there is no obvious person to advocate for younger children like Steven and to help them, gradually, to interpret their home environment and adults' behaviour towards them. Grandparents and members of the extended family can often fulfil the role of advocate or provider of respite, but in this family, like many others, there are no supportive friends or relations.

The assessment of Steven's needs made with his mother and with a better understanding of Steven himself might determine that he would fare better in a day nursery than in a playgroup, taking advantage of the expertise offered by staff at a day nursery or family centre. Centres like these would work with Steven's difficult behaviour and offer support and encouragement to his mother and sister.

If the request for a service were denied but Steven's mother somehow found the means and energy to send him to the local playgroup, Steven's behaviour could make him too difficult for the volunteers who ran the playgroup to manage or for the other children to tolerate. He could find himself labelled as a bully instead of his behaviour being understood from within the context of his experiences at home. Steven could be excluded from playgroup until he went to school at the age of 5. This would leave him without respite from the tensions at home and without access to the consistent responses that a good-quality nursery provides. The 'highscope' research in America has demonstrated how quality nursery provision can mitigate against a range of adversities for children and provide them with better opportunities in later life (Sinclair 1993).

Melanie and Steven's referrals could, at first sight, be regarded as straightforward, not complex and not needing particular skills. They are the type of referral social work students could cut their professional teeth on. Yet referrals like these need careful assessment, which can involve work with a pre-school child as well as older children. They can provide the opportunity for good preventive work that might forestall a later referral of significant or likely significant harm.

Working with children in need of protection

The process of work with children in need of protection will be examined in the early stages of enquiries leading up to and including the child protection conference. The case studies used include those of a 5-year-old and a 15-year-old child.

Some children and young people in need of protection are able to be as involved as their parents in these early stages of the work. Children whose parents are not able to provide reliable consistent care for a variety of reasons (which may include mental or physical ill-health, drug or alcohol misuse, or serious learning disabilities) may be prematurely responsible for their parents' welfare and their own well-being. At times when the parents are least able to make decisions, professionals will be considering what is in the child's best interests. This should, wherever possible, be taking place with the help of other relatives or important family friends. Children and young people in these circumstances need to be fully informed and involved without bearing additional inappropriate responsibility.

CASE STUDY

Keith is 5 and moved with his mother from Scotland to the south of England 6 months ago. The two live in bed and breakfast accommodation, having recently been evicted from a privately rented furnished flat. Keith refused to go home with his mother who was drunk when she came to collect her son from school. The teacher had seen how frightened Keith had become when his mother collected him in a drunken state. This was becoming a very regular occurrence. The teacher has noticed that his work and concentration at school have both deteriorated and has been told by Keith that he is often left alone when his mother goes out drinking. Keith has no other family or family friends living locally, and his mother has been estranged from all her family in Scotland since before Keith's birth.

The excessive intake of alcohol or drugs increases the likelihood of parents being unable to meet their children's needs and carries a risk of abuse and neglect (Hill *et al.* 1996; Reder *et al.* 1993; Christensen 1997). Since most treatment is aimed at the adult drinkers, the children's problems are frequently overlooked. Schools are in a key position to notice the harm that children may suffer and can trigger a referral for support or protection. The highest proportion of child protection referrals, other than those coming from relatives, are those made by teachers who, as in Keith's case, have picked up on the child's distress. The skill and sensitivity of school-based staff such as teachers, counsellors or school nurses will make a difference to the extent to which the child is allowed to have an influence in these first contacts in the child protection process (Schofield and Thoburn 1996:34).

The first task in Keith's case is to determine whether or not emergency action needs to be taken to protect him. In these circumstances, a 5-year-old's wishes not to go home are likely to be taken very seriously. If his mother does not consent to accommodation, it may be necessary to gain an Emergency Protection Order to prevent him being taken home. Keith's mother reluctantly agrees to Keith being accommodated, although the following day, when she has sobered up, she takes Keith home.

Ascertainining wishes and feelings

Keith had said he did not want to go home with his mother. Now, a day later, she is insisting he come with her and Keith says he wants to go with his mother. Keith will be allowed to go home with his mother unless being in her care today is seen to amount to significant harm, in which case an application will be made to the court for an Emergency

Protection Order. Keith needs the opportunity to talk to the social worker alone about whether he feels safe enough to go home, and if he says 'no', it will be important to allow him to remain in foster care. It is probably true that Keith does want to be with his mother since most children do want to be with their family, but this is not necessarily in his best interests. Considering whether his wishes tally with his best interests will be a continuous part of the process.

Building a picture of his wishes and feelings will need to be done over time; finding out once is never enough. Although Keith is a very articulate child, it will also be important to use play and some direct techniques with him. The worry bee exercise (see Chapter 3) could elicit some of Keith's own concerns. Children living with alcohol-abusing parents often feel angry, frightened and upset (Hill *et al.* 1996), and finding the specifics of Keith's concerns may help the worker to allay some of his anxieties, even at this very early stage. It will also help to build up the assessment of significant harm for the conference, where concerns about Keith and the parenting he receives will be shared by the professionals who know him.

All the work that is done with Keith will need to acknowledge the level of responsibility he has held as a very young child for his parent and for himself. A child's sense of responsibility will not be banished by the separation from a parent. Indeed, there may be an enhanced sense of anxiety about the parent's well-being. Because of this, children like Keith who may be separated from a parent need frequent contact and very regular phone calls even at this very early stage so the child can know how the parent is. Although Keith was separated for only one night, he insisted on telephone contact with his mother that night to be reassured about his mother's safety.

As the work with Keith has progressed, he has said that he wants to live with his mother but that he wants her to stop drinking. Any plans to help his mother with her drinking need to recognise the effects not only of the drinking on Keith, but also of any treatment. Children are an important part of the equation in treatment and support for parents, and often become marginalised from the process. Groups where Keith could meet other children living in similar circumstances may be helpful (Christensen 1997). Keith has also said that he wants to stay at the same school. He has clearly made a good and trusting relationship with his teacher, and it will be particularly important to encourage his mother to enable him to keep the continuity of school and this relationship both during the stressful process of enquiries and at a later date when the flurry of activity surrounding the child has died down.

Participation at the child protection conference

It is not essential for Keith to be present at the conference for his views to be represented. As Barford and Wattam comment:

> Children need to become fully involved, knowledgable, and participate throughout the whole child protection process, before they could really be seen as effective conference participants, at which point consideration of their participation may seem almost an irrelevance. (Barford and Wattam 1991:98)

Even when children participate at conferences and appear to be fully involved, they are often only partially aware of what is happening and their own role in the process (Shepherd 1994; Shemmings 1996). Good preparation is a key to successful child participation at meetings, whether they attend in person or have their views represented. Because Keith has been listened to and heard, he is likely to trust a worker to represent his views alongside his mother. After the conference, Keith will need to know what decisions have been made that will affect him and how his views have been acted on. Will he be able to stay at the same school? Will his mother stop drinking? He will need reassurance, help and support throughout his childhood, whether or not he stays at home with his mother.

Different family problems and dilemmas were raised in Fatima's case, although the child protection process followed a similar pattern.

CASE STUDY

Fatima, a 15-year-old Muslim girl of Algerian origin, was beaten by her father when he learnt she had been seeing a boy and missing school. This was a matter of great shame to the family, who felt their daughter would be thought of as a whore. After the beating, Fatima attempted to run away from home but was pursued by her family. The police and social services intervened when a violent family row broke out in public. She refused to go home and was accommodated by the local authority at her own request and against the wishes of her parents. The family were outraged that outside professionals were brought in to regulate their family life and felt that they knew best how to protect and promote their daughter's interests. Fatima and her family have lived in the UK for 4 years. Fatima's command of English is excellent, but her parents' use of the language is very limited.

At the pre-enquiry stage, Fatima was able to talk in confidence to the police and social worker who interviewed her about the assault. She felt they listened to her and took her seriously:

> They asked me what happened, I explained it. I knew they'd listened because then afterwards they asked me questions about what I'd said.

Fatima was also consulted and involved in the choice of a foster family, but she went home at her own request after three nights because the freedom offered to her in this family felt alien and wrong compared with her restricted home life.

Ascertaining wishes and feelings

As with Keith, the role with Fatima as the child protection enquiries continue includes gathering information about significant harm and ascertaining Fatima's wishes and feelings. These are to be presented at the child protection conference. In this instance, Fatima attended the conference herself and voiced her own views.

Fatima was cognitively and emotionally mature but confused about the competing cultural demands of her family and the Western culture at school, which offered more of a say to children. Fatima quickly concluded that her wishes were to abide by her family's beliefs and accept a restricted lifestyle. Some things, however, she felt she would not accept:

> My dad needs to understand that he can't beat up his children. In the area where my dad grew up it was different so my dad believes in hitting children. All I want him to understand is that it's not right.

Where there is a conflict between what an adolescent wants and what the family wants, it is imperative not only that social workers assess the young person's level of maturity, but also that work is done with them to try to ensure they understand the implications of rejecting the customs and religious practices of their childhood (Department of Health 1996b:17).

Work with children from Muslim families underlines the need for particular sensitivity about cultural values. Sinclair *et al.*'s (1995) study showed that working with Muslim families posed problems for social workers, who often had little or no prior experience of working with this particular religious group. They noted a lack of confidence in the social workers that led to tensions, misunderstandings and mistrust:

The parents' inability to compromise over certain things, such as their daughter's dress, social life, and particularly boyfriends, made it hard for us to do any meaningful work with them. We were very ignorant though... Given their cultural background it was clear that we had totally unrealistic expectations of them. (Sinclair *et al.* 1995:105)

Participation at the child protection conference

Fatima attended the conference alongside her parents and made her feelings known to the meeting. She had been given good information about the format of the meeting and how she could contribute:

> I was at the conference and they did ask me all the time if I wanted to say something and they did involve me. I'm glad that they involved me and wanted to hear what I had to say. I wanted to hear what they were saying about me.

Summary of the work with Fatima

Fatima was guarded in her resonses to the worker, and the relationship that developed was always distant. Yet Fatima was able to voice her views, get the help she needed and control the intensity of the involvement. She used the worker to help her become clear about what she wanted in a way that kept intrusions into her family life to a minimum. The case was closed within 2 months of the conference. The beating at home had stopped, but in other respects Fatima's life at home had not changed. However, this was acceptable to Fatima, who wanted to live by the customs and ways of her family. In Fatima's case, there was ultimately no conflict between her wishes and her parents wishes; she agreed to abide by their cultural codes.

Conclusion

This chapter has covered the circumstances surrounding early work with children in need and children in need of protection. Many problems for the child are rooted in parental difficulties such as mental ill-health, domestic violence or substance abuse. Work with children in these contexts should always aim to understand how the child feels and keep in mind the child's perspective. It should also look to future supports for the child. Once enquiries have been completed and services offered, the case will often be closed and the work with the child will cease. It is important that the child gains a good experience through her contacts with the social worker.

Children need to know why a social worker is visiting them. They need to know about services they can use and how they can gain access to them. They need to know about decisions that have been made which will affect them. A social worker who has listened, explained and understood will make a child feel that she can come back for help. The child may seek that help from social services or may feel more confident in approaching professionals in more everyday settings such as school and health centres.

Further reading

Butler, I. and Williamson, H. (1994) *Children Speak: Children, Trauma and Social Work* (London: NSPCC/Longman).

A study of the views of 190 young people mostly over 10 years of age, about half of whom had had some contact with social services. Its aim was 'to shed light on young people's feelings and perspectives on issues such as "worst experiences", anxieties, adult support and professional intervention'.

Epstein, C. and Keep, G. (1995) In Saunders, A. *It Hurts Me Too: Children's Experiences of Domestic Violence and Refuge Life* (London: WAFE/ NISW/ChildLine).

A book containing three separate pieces about children's experiences of domestic violence and the help they have received from sources as diverse as ChildLine and Women's Refuges.

Schofield, G. and Thoburn, J. (1996) *Child Protection: The Voice of the Child in Decision Making* (London: Institute for Public Policy Research).

A thorough review of the literature on the subject and a detailed account of children's involvement throughout the child protection process.

Shemmings, D. (1996) *Children's Involvment in Child Protection Conferences*, Social Work Monograph (Norwich: University of East Anglia).

5

Children who are the Subject of Care and Adoption Proceedings in the Courts

Introduction

The very thought of 'court' is extremely daunting, even to most adults. For children, images of court are generally based on television and are mostly frightening. The idea of a formal court room in which judges look down from a great height, most commonly when deciding how to punish criminals, is one that is familiar to all of us. For social workers as well as children, coming into contact with a court may shake their confidence. For children whose future is to be decided in the courts, there is very great anxiety about what will happen next, whom they will live with and all the important details of their lives that may change following the court's decision. Social workers therefore need to be very clear about the court system, the options available and their various roles during proceedings involving children. They also need to be very aware of the impact of the process on children as well as the outcome. Their confidence and concern will be communicated to the child.

This chapter will focus on children involved in care and adoption proceedings. It will consider what social work skills may be required to assist children through the court process and to limit the stress that the system itself, although setting out to work in children's best interests, will almost inevitably cause them.

Legal and institutional framework: care and related proceedings

There are a range of applications that would lead to a child being the subject of care and related proceedings under the Children Act 1989 (see box). These applications are primarily made by the local authority, although there will be some, such as the application by a relative for a Residence Order in respect of a child in care, that are made by family members. All applications involve a major decision about the welfare of the child, and the consequences of these decisions will affect a child's life in profound ways, determining who is to hold parental responsibility, who is to have contact, where the child may live and so on.

APPLICATIONS IN CARE AND RELATED PROCEEDINGS

- Emergency Protection Order (s.44)
- Child Assessment Order (s.43)
- Care or Supervision Order (s.31)
- contact with a child who is subject of a Care Order (s.34)
- Residence Order application where child is subject to a Care Order (s.8)
- applications to discharge a Care Order, vary or discharge Supervision Orders.

The number of children coming before the courts is a very small proportion of the number of children who are referred to social services departments. Recent figures suggest that of approximately 160,000 children referred to child protection agencies in a year, only 3,000 children become subject to care orders (Department of Health 1995). These figures appear to reflect the philosophy of the Children Act 1989 that courts will only become involved where children continue to suffer or are likely to suffer significant harm in spite of the provision of family support services and an interagency child protection plan. Although the detail of practice varies from authority to authority (Thoburn *et al.* 1996), children who are the subject of care proceedings applications will be deemed by the local authority to be suffering or likely to suffer significant harm. Children are therefore likely to have suffered some degree of abuse or neglect and are likely to have developmental problems. A number of these children will have parents who suffer from a range of additional problems that affect their ability to parent, such as mental health problems, learning difficulties, drug and alcohol misuse.

In the majority of applications for Care or Supervision Orders, an application will follow a period of working with a family to prevent the need for intervention through the court, and much will be known about the child and the family. If there has been good social work practice during the family support and child protection work, much should also be known about the child's perspective on events in the family and the application itself. Because the application is by the local authority and the key worker within the child protection system will have been the social worker, the social worker will play a key role in the process of taking the case to court. This will include taking legal advice from the local authority solicitor and also formally giving instructions on behalf of the social services department.

In each of these applications mentioned above, the child has the status of a party to proceedings, which gives entitlement to legal representation by a solicitor. Also in these proceedings, a guardian ad litem will be appointed. These two participants in the court process play very different yet complementary roles in representing the child's interests, wishes and feelings. The social worker, who also has responsibilities for the child's welfare and for communicating the child's wishes and feelings to the court, will therefore need to work alongside the guardian and the child's solicitor and remain clear about the distinctive local authority social work role.

The social worker works not only within the framework of the law but also within the practice guidance associated with the Children Act 1989. Now that the Act is no longer 'new', it is rare for social workers to look on a regular basis at such documents as *Care of Children: Principles and Practice in Regulations and Guidance* (Department of Health 1989), yet these contain extremely useful lessons for practice. Furthermore, the importance of the social worker's understanding of research knowledge, prior to making applications but particularly in formulating care plans that include consideration of the child's wishes and feelings, cannot be overestimated (see especially *Patterns and Outcomes in Child Placement: Messages from Current Research and their Implications* (Department of Health 1991a) and *Child Protection: Messages from Research* (Dartington Social Research Unit 1995).

Legal and institutional framework: adoption proceedings

Although only a small number of children will be involved in adoption proceedings, this is an important area of work, if only because the decisions that will be made are possibly the most far-reaching of all for the child – to legally end the parental responsibility of a birth parent and invest it in an adoptive parent. Adoption was not part of the review of legislation that went into the Children Act 1989 but has been subsequently the subject of a lengthy review and consultation process as a prelude to legislation. However, even under existing legislation (Adoption Act 1976 s.1), there is an expectation that the Schedule 2 report, prepared by the social worker, must include an account of the wishes and feelings of the child. It is of great concern that, in spite of this requirement, a research study found that children's views were not recorded in half of the sampled reports, (Selwyn 1996).

Although the circumstances of the court application and the legislative process are very different from those of care proceedings, the levels of anxiety and the uncertainty of the outcome, which can last for many months, will, from the child's point of view, have aspects in common. The need for the child to feel consulted and involved in the process is also characteristic of both kinds of proceedings. The principles of the social work task will therefore also be that work on behalf of the child must be accompanied by work with the child to ensure that the child is able to make sense of what is happening, can express his wishes and feelings and is emotionally supported in coping with the process.

Applications by children

Children may also, with leave of the court, make certain applications, such as for contact or residence, in their own right. This was seen as one of the most radical features of the Children Act, and there was a great deal of media comment about the child's right to 'divorce' her parents. In practice, the courts have taken a cautious approach to applications by children, including making a ruling that children's applications could only be made in the High Court. It is not clear what impact the issue of children's own applications will have on child protection. Application for a s.8 Residence Order by a child wishing to live with a grandparent or for a s.8 or s.34 Contact Order in the course of care proceedings are certainly possible. In the following example, it was possible for the social worker to assist a young person through the process of making an application.

CASE STUDY

Patrick (aged 15) was in the care of the local authority. He wanted contact with his younger siblings who were living at home but was refusing to have contact with his father because his father had threatened and upset him during a previous unsupervised contact. His father would not allow the sibling contact and the situation drifted, with Patrick feeling very isolated. With the social worker's assistance, Patrick was put in touch with a solicitor who had acted for him before. He instructed a solicitor to make a s.8 application for contact with his siblings. His father responded with a s.34 application in an attempt to force the local authority to arrange contact between himself and his son. The court proceedings initiated by the child led to a resolution of the situation by negotiation, Patrick having contact with his siblings and also contact, although supervised at his request, with his father (Schofield and Thoburn 1996).

Context of the work with the child

Before considering in more depth the social worker's role in relation to face-to-face work with the child during proceedings, it is important to consider the context of the work during proceedings. Work with the child is not conducted in a vacuum. On the contrary, so much else is going on that work with the child can too often get overlooked. Much is expected of social workers during court proceedings, which is not surprising. It is the local authority's application that has brought the matter to court, so the social worker's role as the central figure is inevitable.

Although the detail of that role will vary depending on the nature of the proceedings, there will be a number of common tasks:

● managing the court application
● being a caseworker for the family
● liaising with other agencies.

Managing the court application

The social worker for the child will be responsible for managing many aspects of the court application and can often feel as if the court system is taking over their professional role with the family. Most social workers agree that it is the mass of administrative work associated with court proceedings which makes it hard at times to give the child the time that is needed. This is not only in the obvious areas of report-writing for court, but often also in making arrangements for contact, for children and family members to get to assessments, for medical examinations and so on. Because this work will potentially be subject to the scrutiny of the courts as well as of the agency, this can be a source of additional stress.

In particular, social workers can feel that they become answerable to the local authority legal department not only for court deadlines, but also for aspects of their professional practice and decision-making. It is therefore very important that the worker for the child makes a clear distinction between the need for legal advice from the local authority solicitor and the ability to make professional judgements about the child's welfare, instructing the solicitor accordingly. The decision as to whether the local authority believes the child to be at risk of significant harm, for example, is a professional decision, although it is helpful to be advised of legal precedents and to be clear about the nature of 'evidence'.

Social workers' obligation to children is to pursue what they feel to be in the child's best interests, following consultation with professional colleagues in all disciplines. Part of this obligation will, of course, be to meet deadlines with competent reports, to prepare care plans that reflect a considered view of the child's welfare, wishes and feelings, and to present evidence clearly in court.

The impact of delay on the child needs also to be taken into account. When care proceedings are initiated, it is the beginning of a process that is likely to last anything from 4 to 6 months – and in some cases up to a year. Although, when the Children Act was implemented, the avoidance of delay was seen as so critical that it was built in to the Act itself (s.1.2), the originally hoped-for length of proceedings has rarely been achieved in practice. Whether the delays are felt to be constructive or harmful in the long run, from the child's point of view this period of time for the court to make a decision about her future seems unending and incomprehensible. Whatever the outcome for the child of court proceedings, it would be unrealistic to think that it will be achieved without some cost to her. The social worker must minimise delay where possible, but where it is inevitable or possibly constructive, she must set aside time to help the child cope with what will be a stressful period.

Being a caseworker for the family

The role of parents and other family members in the child protection system has been radically changed since the late 1980s following research on the benefits of parental participation (Thoburn *et al.* 1995). Social work in partnership with parents and the participation of parents at case conferences have become accepted as good practice, and there are guidelines to assist practitioners (Department of Health 1995). These principles will, of course, continue to operate when children become the subject of care proceedings. The work with the child will therefore be within the context of work with parents, who continue to retain parental responsibility when a care order or interim care order is in force. This will have a number of implications, whether the child is at home or in foster or residential care. It will be necessary to keep parents informed of all aspects of the child's welfare if they are separated from the family, and parents will need to have the opportunity to discuss with the social worker the work which is done with the child. This may be a delicate process of negotiation. Parents facing court proceedings may be concerned that their child is going to be unduly influenced or even put under pressure by substitute carers, social workers or other professionals, such as child psychiatrists, who are talking to their children in confidence.

The process of negotiation with parents around the work with the child deserves proper attention. Parents have a right to know what is going to be the focus of the work and to express a view about that. However, the child also has the right to have the opportunity to share her feelings and express her views through the social worker. The skill of the social worker lies in enabling both parents and children to understand the need for the social worker to speak separately with the child and to feel comfortable with that. Confrontations in which parents or social workers attempt to overrule the other will lead to the child feeling confused and uncertain. This will undermine any attempt to build a relationship of trust.

Liaising with other agencies

Child care social workers are already very much aware of the need for interagency collaboration in order to share information and provide appropriate services to children and families during the child protection process. Social workers will also need to ensure that good communication links are established during the court process so that they are up to date with changing events that occur in the system. What is more, the social worker will need to ensure that the child remains the focus of attention when interagency decisions are to be made. Court proceedings can create a great deal of anxiety in interagency networks, and if this leads to conflict and poor communication, the social worker may need to be sure that she is keeping the child in mind and ensuring that others are doing likewise.

As the social worker plans his or her own work with the child, it will be important to ensure that other agencies and carers are informed of the work to be undertaken. All agencies will be aware that a child's wishes and feelings must be ascertained, and it may be necessary to clarify which of the professionals involved will take the lead role in the work with the child. All professionals will have their own idea of the child's views from their different kinds of contact. Where children are attending a family centre, having art therapy, relating to numerous staff at school and seeing a child psychiatrist for assessment – in addition to contact with the social worker – there is a need to ensure that the child is not overwhelmed by competing and perhaps conflicting attempts to establish what the child 'really' wants.

Work with the child during proceedings

The following are key tasks for the social worker with the child during proceedings:

- establishing principles for the work
- offering emotional support
- making sense of the court process
- preparing for/discussing consent to expert assessments
- making a developmental assessment
- ascertaining the child's wishes and feeling
- facilitating participation.

Establishing principles for the work

In what may be a changing and complex world, it will be helpful for the child to hang on to a clear sense of the worker's role, what work it is proposed to do with the child during proceedings and in what timescale. This is not easy to do, given the uncertain timing of interim court hearings, interagency meetings, contact arrangements and so on. However, if, at the outset, basic expectations are laid down as a commitment to the child, there can be some allowance made for changes as the case proceeds. A framework or set of principles for the working relationship between the worker and the child during proceedings can be by an agreement, which may be oral or written depending on the age of the child. These are some of the principles which should be considered.

- *Confidentiality.* The social worker is not able to offer total confidentiality, because of the concerns that have led to the court proceedings and the nature of the court proceedings. Nevertheless, any information that needs to be shared with others should only be passed to those who need to know; for example, the teacher may not need to know to know that a child is bedwetting. This information would not be available about other children in the class. This process will in itself be discussed with the child.

- *Reliability.* The social worker should visit at minimum intervals during proceedings, perhaps fortnightly. The frequency will depend a great deal on the child's circumstances, at times being more or less frequent. It is most important that the child knows what to expect.

- *Direct communication.* The social worker should communicate directly with the child where possible. This needs to be carefully negotiated. If the child is in foster or residential care, it will be important to check with carers when it is convenient to visit – but then the worker can either ask to speak to or drop a line to the child rather than asking for the message to be passed on. Similarly, if the worker has to change any arrangements, it can make a difference if contact has been made directly with the child, even when the child may have had the information already from elsewhere.

- *Availability.* The child needs to know how to contact the social worker. Children ought to be given a card with telephone numbers and, if looked after, have access to a confidential phone. This is part of the standard requirements for children's homes but is not always available in foster homes. Older children may need to have money to phone the social worker from a phone box as needed. This is not to be seen as a way of marginalising the main carers – the child should of course be encouraged to feel able to talk to carers – but it simply recognises that children need to know that the key worker is directly available for them.

- *Consultation.* The social worker should consult the child before all decisions are made. Again, there needs to be clarity about this. Children need to understand that there will be different kinds of decision and that, although their views on all of them will be listened to, in some their views, such as where contact should take place, may play a major role, whereas in others, such as returning home when there is still a serious risk, those wishes may be overruled.

- *Participation.* There will be a need to clarify how the social worker will be helping the child to participate. Will this involve the child attending certain meetings or court hearings? Will it mean preparing a statement for court? If the child is wary of the social services department, is there an independent advocate available?

- *Plans.* The social worker will ensure that all possible options are made available to the child in a form that the child can understand. This may mean using toys or diagrams or whatever materials the child is most comfortable with. Once plans are agreed, the child should know what they are and, for children of appropriate age and understanding, have their own copy in writing.

- *Beginnings and endings.* Planning for the end of a working relation-ship should begin, where possible, at the beginning. The child needs to know what to expect from the relationship and the worker so that both will know when the work is finished and the relationship will end. This should give some indication to the child of the role the social worker will play in her life. For example, if the worker is in a short-term team that hands over cases after the court has made its decision, the child should know this at the beginning. It does not necessarily mean that the child will trust the worker with less of herself; it is more important that the child knows what to expect.

There is a simple reason for this degree of care being taken with the detail and principles of the relationship between the worker and the child. Treating children with respect and sensitivity does not simply help the child to survive the process – it is essentially therapeutic in itself. Children can benefit from a predictable and personal relation-ship in the middle of a process that can feel unpredictable and impersonal. It can also help the child who may have felt devalued or rejected to begin to regain her self-respect.

Offering emotional support

Where children are at home, they will need support with what may be a very difficult situation. Children may feel under pressure from both family members and professionals. Children who are separated from their family following child protection concerns will be trying to cope with their own complex feelings about the separation. Children in both circumstances face uncertainty through the courts, and there will be a significant need to experience some sense of emotional support.

For children at home, this may come from the continuity of relationships at school with peers and teachers. For looked-after children, this may also be the case, but some sense of security should also come from the day-to-day, reliable, concerned care of foster carers or residential workers. Nevertheless, the social worker will still have an important role to play. This may be because there has been a pre-existing relationship with the worker and the worker therefore represents continuity. If the worker knew the child before the court process began, this is important to children who feel disconnected from their past selves. For looked-after children, the social worker will effectively be the child's link with home.

Making sense of the court process

The challenge for social workers in their work with children involved in court proceedings is to operate in a way which bridges the gap between the world of the law and the courts, and the world of the child. Even more than in other areas of social work practice with children, enabling the child to make sense of events requires skill and patience, the ability to work with the child at the child's pace and the use of strategies that are appropriate to the child's age and understanding. It is important not to use language or concepts that cannot be understood and that merely add to anxieties. It is equally important not to underestimate the capacity of children to grasp the essential nature of the court process, and even quite young children, certainly by 6 or 7 years of age, can be helped to make some sense of the decisions being made about them.

Although emotional support is important, it is likely that part of the strategy for helping the child to cope with her anxieties will be to enable her to gain as much knowledge and understanding as is possible or appropriate of the court system and the associated processes of assessment, expert evidence and representation through the guardian ad litem and the solicitor. Although workers may wish to protect the child from such knowledge or feel that such knowledge is unnecessary or inappropriate for young children in particular, they need to remember all the ways in which the child will be drawn in. For example, the child needs to be prepared quite carefully for the visit of the guardian ad litem. If the social worker can let the child know the name of the person – perhaps the social worker has already met her and can reassure the child – it allows the child to start to picture what this person with the strange sounding job might be like.

The very fact that the court system is so alien to the child's sense of familiar things means that social workers will need to use all the skills at their disposal for communicating to the child a useful way of understanding the process. For most children, words will simply not be enough. With very young children, perhaps aged 4 or 5, it may be helpful to use soft toys to set up in front of the child a construction of the decision-making process – the three magistrates, the social worker talking to the court about the child, the parents there with their solicitor to help them and so on. This may not be a single session but could be done at intervals during the proceedings so that it becomes a tool for communicating about the process. There is a video pack produced by the Department of Health called *You Are Not Alone* (Department of Health 1995), which introduces children to the court process and the various professionals involved. Even for teenagers, drawn outlines of what the court looks like, where people sit and so on will be helpful. All children will need help in understanding the different responsibilities of social workers and team leaders, guardians and solicitors, psychiatrists and psychologists. Some children may wish to be taken to see the court building and the court room itself. This will depend very much on the child and also on the court. In most cases, court rooms used for family proceedings have been made more informal, and it may help the child to think of 'court' as being people sitting around a table. On the other hand, some care centre courts, for example, are in the same building as the crown courts. This may mean armed security officers being around during certain criminal trials.

Preparation for/discussing consent to expert assessments

All children will need help in understanding specific aspects of the court process, such as the court's requirement for assessments. Although it may seem that young children should not be expected to understand the role of a psychiatrist, for example, it is necessary to prepare the child for such assessments. At the very least, the child needs to understand that the psychiatrist, although called 'doctor', is not going to examine her physically to see whether she is ill. The child should know whether she is going to be playing with toys or sitting in a family meeting. The child may particularly need to know whether the assessment session is to include a specific parent or other family members. For some children, this presence will be a reassuring, positive factor, for others a source of anxiety. Either way, the child, who may be taken out of school and may travel to a distant clinic, should have some idea of what to expect. Because of this need to prepare the child, it is important for there to be contact between the social worker and the professionals involved in the assessment to establish the exact nature of the assessment process. This is important in any event to keep the social worker informed of how the case is developing, but it additionally tells the social worker not just the terms of reference of the assessment, but also what practically the child can expect to happen.

The child's involvement in discussion about assessments is necessary also because, under the Children Act 1989, the child who is of 'sufficient understanding to make an informed decision' (s.38) has the right to refuse to submit to medical or psychiatric examinations as directed by the court. It is likely that, although the court may look to the guardian ad litem to assist in determining whether the child passes this test of competence to refuse consent, the social worker, who is likely to know the child best, has a role to play in discussing with the child her feelings about the proposed assessment and should be able to contribute to a discussion about competence and consent.

The nature of 'informed' consent in child protection situations is complex. Where the implications of a positive finding of physical or sexual abuse may lead to the possibility of a child being separated from her family and a parent facing criminal charges, it is difficult for the child to weigh up the balance between the risk of continuing to live in a familiar but abusive situation, and the possibility of living somewhere strange but safe.

For older children, it can be very important to feel that an examination is being carried out with their consent. As with other areas of children's participation in child protection work, children who have felt powerless in an abusive situation will benefit from feeling some sense of control over events in their lives.

CASE STUDY

Jane, a fourteen year old with learning difficulties was recently referred for a medical examination in relation to sexual abuse allegations. In the waiting room, she was saying to the social worker over and over again, 'The guardian from the court says I don't have to have this examination if I don't want to. It's OK for me to change my mind, even at the last minute.' The social worker confirmed that this was the case. Jane went ahead with the examination but felt that it had to some extent at least been her choice (Schofield and Thoburn 1996:54).

Those working with young people need to be aware that, although there is always anxiety about the implications of a child refusing to submit to an examination, there is a benefit to the child in organising the situation in a way which provides the opportunity for the child to express a view and feel some sense of control of her body.

The position that has been established in judgements since the Children Act appears to be that the child's refusal to consent can still be overruled by anyone with parental responsibility or by a court. However, this does not mean that children's views should not be taken fully into account and their consent sought as the Act intended. As elsewhere in relation to participation, the process can be as important as the outcome.

Making a developmental assessment

Even where there has previously been an assessment of the child's welfare and development, the regular contact during court proceedings allows the worker to continue to assess the child and to determine the extent to which the child appears to be developing within the normal range or whether there is cause for concern in any of the areas identified under the Children Act 1989 (s.31) definition of significant harm. Much of this information will have to be checked with specialists, such as the speech therapist, the community paediatrician or the educational psychologist. Such an ongoing assessment is useful in defining the risk to the child, but it also enables the worker to start to develop a picture of children's experiences within all areas of their life, their strengths and weaknesses, their life within the family or the school or the neighbourhood. This will then contribute to the formulation of the care plan, which must address needs and risks.

Ascertaining the child's wishes and feelings

This is a major area of work with the child in all aspects of child care decision-making. In the court setting, however, because the child's wishes and feelings are a part of the welfare checklist (Children Act

1989, s.1.3) to be considered by the court before making a decision, it needs particular and explicit attention. The fact that the welfare of the child is paramount is a principle easily understood and shared by all parties to the proceedings, however different their views of the child's best interests may be. The role of the child's voice in decision-making in court is much less clear. The question of the weight to be given to children's views raises very strong feelings in all arenas, but in courts, where decisions can affect the rest of their childhood, all professionals involved in a case and those who will ultimately make those decisions – the magistrates and judges – will struggle to get it 'right'. In practice, court decisions are never simple, and it is likely that a range of options are available, each of which will meet some but not all of a child's needs and some but not all of her wishes. Wishes themselves can be complex and contradictory for children, as they often are for parents and professionals. Let us take the case of Maria as an example.

CASE STUDY

Maria is fourteen years old and is the eldest child of three siblings, two sisters and a brother. She has been sexually abused, as have her siblings, by a series of men. This is not in dispute. She is subject of care proceedings. Her wishes look like this:

- I want to live with my mother BUT I want not to be afraid when men come to the house and I have to run away.
- I love my Mum and I don't want her to be lonely BUT I want the abuse to stop and she keeps choosing boyfriends who hurt us.
- I don't want to have smelly clothes because then other children are horrible to me BUT I don't want to be different from other children by being in care.
- I don't want to be in foster care with foster carers telling me what to do BUT I don't want to be at home and hear my brother scream when he's being abused (Schofield and Thoburn 1996:18).

This is a fairly typical list of contradictory wishes that a child may have after a childhood in which abuse and mixed messages from parents have left her troubled and confused. Of course, the child does not produce a list in this form or in one session. Some days,

Maria might be clearer about certain wishes rather than others. The key point here is that it is not possible for Maria to be safe *and* at home. Therefore, by definition, it is not possible for the court to make a decision that will satisfy all of her expressed wishes, even if it wanted to. Parents, and indeed social workers, will also have lists of wishes for the child that will contain mutually exclusive and incompatible elements, just as the child's list does. Wanting Maria to be safe and happy without experiencing any further distress or upset is not possible. To suggest that the issue before the court is to balance the child's wish to go home, the one most clearly articulated, with the need to protect her would underestimate the complexity of the situation. To suggest that 'Maria says she wants to go home but she doesn't mean it' is equally unhelpful and shows a lack of appreciation of the child's attempt to reconcile what are clearly incompatible wishes. This is not an exceptional case. A child's natural wish to be at home, but for it to be different, must be the most commonly expressed wish and the most difficult to satisfy. Courts must be helped by experts in the field, including social workers, to understand this.

Given the complexity of the child's wishes and feelings, the process of ascertaining them is not a simple one. As earlier chapters have demonstrated, the age and understanding of the child, the impact of abuse or neglect and the impact of the investigation itself are all factors that will affect the work of the social worker with the child. Maria was, at the time of proceedings, upset at the separation from her mother but seemed a different child as she responded to a period of safety and reliable care from her foster carers. Courts should expect to have evidence that all efforts have been made to enable children to communicate their wishes and feelings but will also need to understand the other factors that may have contributed to the child's state of mind.

Even in emergency proceedings, it should be possible in some cases to ascertain the child's wishes and feelings. When the decision is made, sometimes at a child protection conference or occasionally by the local authority alone, to apply to the court for an Emergency Protection Order, time needs to be taken by the social worker to consider the impact of this application on the child and the appropriate ways in which the child's wishes and feelings can be ascertained. Although the welfare checklist does not have to be legally taken into account when the court considers the making of an Emergency Protection Order, it is set out in s.22(4a) of the Children Act 1989 that:

before making any decision with respect to a child whom they are looking after, or proposing to look after, a local authority shall, so far as is reasonably practicable, ascertain the wishes and feelings of the child.

It may seem as if such an expectation is difficult to put into effect given the likely circumstances of an Emergency Protection Order but, as in other areas of social work practice with children, how events begin sets a tone for the child and gives her messages about what to expect in the future. If the message to the child at the outset is that court proceedings are beyond her control and that children are simply objects to be moved around according to the decisions of powerful adults outside the family, it may be more difficult subsequently to establish a culture in which the child is a valued and active participant in discussions about her own future. The advantage of early participation is also that regardless of the decision that is made in terms of an order, certain views of the child can be established at the beginning.

CASE STUDY

A decision is made at a child protection conference that Ellen, an eleven year old girl who has been physically and sexually abused, will not be safe to remain at home because of the visits of the alleged abuser to the home. The mother denies the possibility of current abuse although there is medical evidence. A decision is made to apply for an emergency protection order on the grounds that applying for an interim care order under notice would leave the child at considerable risk. The application is to be heard later that day. Ellen is seen at school by the social worker who is able to discuss the application with her. Ellen states that she does not wish to leave her mother. She accepts that her mother has been unable to keep this man away in the past but hopes she will change (Schofield and Thoburn 1996:50).

The court is made aware by the social worker of the feelings of the child and the justices may refer to them in their reasons. If they are satisfied of the risk of significant harm and the need for an order, they will be likely to make an Emergency Protection Order. The child's welfare is paramount. Nevertheless, all participants will be made aware of the child's feelings at the outset, particularly about the significance of the relationship between her and her mother. This will put the importance of her views on the agenda for the rest of the proceedings, even if the content of those views should change. Furthermore, she will be entitled to an explanation if those views are overruled.

In care proceedings, care plans that set out the local authority's plans for the future of the child if a Care Order is made have become central. It is a requirement of care plans that the child's wishes and feelings must be recorded and taken into account (Children Act Guidance and Regulations, Volume 3, para 2.62) – and that reasons must be given if the plan diverges from the child's wishes. Again, this requirement is not designed to put pressure on local authorities to follow the child's expressed wishes, but it is necessary to give the message to children and to adults that the child's wishes must be heard and treated with respect.

Facilitating participation

The social worker will need to determine with each child how best to enable the child to participate in the court process and in any plans or agreements, such as around contact, which are made. The need to adapt sensitively to the individual child rather than apply a blanket policy on the nature of participation is similar in court to that found by Shemmings (1996) in relation to participation in case conferences. Some older children will be able and will wish to attend certain meetings and even the court hearings. These children will need extra help to ensure that this is a constructive experience, even where it is also distressing. Most children will need various indirect routes to maximise their involvement. Their wishes and feelings should be communicated to decision-making forums, including the court, as a separate part of the social worker's report. The child may wish to put her wishes and feelings in writing to be read to the court. The child may choose to use the guardian ad litem rather than the social worker as someone who can represent her views in court – but the social worker still has a responsibility as the key worker for the child to ensure that the child is comfortable with whatever arrangements are made for giving and receiving communications during the court process and feeling involved.

The guardian ad litem

Because of the varied nature of the work of child care teams, social workers may only rarely be involved in court work and may not be fully aware of the role and responsibilities of the guardian ad litem. The role of the guardian ad litem was significantly enhanced under the Children Act 1989, and guardians were described by Lady Elizabeth Butler-Sloss as the 'lynch pin of the new legislation'. The court is under a duty to appoint a guardian ad litem in specified proceedings unless satisfied that it is not necessary to do so in order to safeguard the child's interests (s.41(1)). The guardian ad litem plays a key role in proceedings. She provides the court with an independent report that will assist the court in reaching a decision. In addition, the guardian takes responsibility for case management during proceedings and for the avoidance of delay. This involves the guardian in playing an active role in directions hearings, in the process of establishing a timetable and in the decision about the need for expert evidence. It should also be the case that the guardian ensures that both the child's welfare and the child's wishes and feelings are taken into account throughout proceedings rather than only in the final report and final court hearing.

Panels of guardians ad litem and reporting officers are set up and managed primarily by local authorities, although panel members are considered to be independent of the local authority in their work and are responsible to the court. Different employment structures exist in different parts of the country, but all guardians are from social work backgrounds and work within the duties set out in the Children Act 1989 (s.41).

In carrying out her responsibilities, the guardian is entitled to have full access to all local authority files and will interview all those within the family and within the professional network who may be able to contribute information and professional judgements to the guardian's assessment of the situation. Because the guardian is expected to have views about the welfare of the child during proceedings, she has to work quickly but carefully through the available evidence.

A central part of the guardian's work will be to get to know the child and to establish an understanding of her wishes and feelings. The guardian will need to set out a framework and principles for the work with the child. In some respects, these will be similar to those of the social worker, but there are issues arising from the fact that the work is time limited and court focussed. The guardian will also need to use a range of materials to enable the child to communicate her feelings and ideas about her situation. The guardian should be a point of reference throughout proceedings and, where these are long and drawn out and the guardian's visits may be less frequent, the child benefits from active steps being taken to ensure continuity.

Alan (aged 13) was the child of a black African father and a white English mother. He had learning disabilities and attended a weekly boarding school. Care proceedings in relation to allegations of physical and emotional abuse lasted a year in total because of complications involving siblings, expert assessments and a transfer of the case to a higher court. The guardian ad litem used a range of materials with Alan, particularly paper and felt tips and play-dough. She had a special folder with his name on, in which pictures and writing, all dated, were kept. Each time she visited, Alan could pull out the drawings, the lists of wishes and fears, the genograms of his family and so on in order to review his progress over time and his changing preoccupations. Packs of felt tips and pots of play-dough also had his name on and were not used by other children. On one occasion, Alan used the play-dough to create a bird's nest with a mother bird and two baby birds in it. At the end of the session, he placed this carefully in the pot and put the lid on. At the next session, a month later because the guardian had been on leave, he was pleased to be able to retrieve his model unharmed. The message to him was that all that he did and made was sufficiently important for the guardian to look after it between sessions. As with other relationship-based work with children, it reassured him that he was being thought about and cared about. This allowed him to share his difficult and confusing feelings with the guardian in an atmosphere of trust. When the case was finally over, the guardian said goodbye and gave him the materials to keep.

The guardian needs to understand the child's history, both in terms of changes in the child's circumstances, such as moves of house or changes in schools, and in terms of the key relationships, especially significant attachments, in her life. The guardian will also have to consider such issues as race and gender in order to arrive properly at recommendations that meet all the individual child's needs. When arriving at a recommendation that will be in the child's best interests, the guardian will need to be aware of all aspects of the child's health and development as set out under the definition of significant harm (s.31.9). Although it is not the guardian's job formally to investigate allegations of abuse during these sessions with the child, it is quite possible that the child will talk to the guardian about her concerns and may also reveal information about abuse or neglect in her drawings or her play. This may contribute to the guardian's views about the risk of significant harm that the child faces, but it is the court that determines whether or not significant harm has occurred.

Having conducted this often quite comprehensive piece of work through interviews with family members and professionals, and sessions with the child, the guardian will then prepare a report for the final court hearing. This will comment on the range of evidence available to the court, clarifying issues relating to all aspects of the development and welfare of the child. It should also have specific sections on the wishes and feelings of the child, the local authority and the care plan, the welfare checklist – and a final recommendation. After the final hearing, the guardian's role ceases except in the event of an appeal.

Because of the responsibilities of the guardian during proceedings, the working relationship between the local authority social worker and the guardian will be an important one, and both need to be clear about their different but at times overlapping roles. Both derive their expertise from their social work background – although an experienced guardian may have developed more familiarity with court procedures and the experienced social worker is likely to be more familiar with the day-to-day changes in social work practice in the field. Parties during proceedings will be having contact with both the social worker and the guardian, and it is therefore important for the guardian to clarify the ways in which her role is distinctive. Many panels now have leaflets suitable for professionals, family members and children that explain the role of the guardian. Social workers will often be in the position of telling parents or children about the guardian ad litem system and how to contact the particular guardian who has been appointed. It is therefore useful for social workers to familiarise themselves with these leaflets so that there is some consistency between the accounts that parties to proceedings, especially children, will receive.

The most difficult area of overlap to negotiate can be the work with the child. In most cases, the social worker will already have had some contact with the child prior to proceedings, will be able to build on this relationship during proceedings and will have a job to do with the child when implementing the court's decision after the final hearing. The guardian has a much more concentrated piece of work to do – to get to know the child and be able to provide an independent view of the child's welfare and wishes over a brief period and then to say goodbye after the final hearing. Although some duplication is inevitable, such as ensuring that the child understands the court process or checking out the child's feelings about contact, the guardian will not need to take the child to see the court, for example, if the social worker has already done so. In most cases, the roles will need to be negotiated, each accepting that the other also has a job to do. Certainly, overwhelming the child with visits or both visiting on the same day should be avoided. Guardians need to accept that if the social worker has a prior arrangement to see the child, the guardian will need to be flexible. However, if the guardian needs to meet a child immediately before a first hearing, the social worker may need to be flexible. It should not be the case that the guardian takes automatic priority, as sometimes happens.

During the proceedings, the social worker will need to keep the guardian informed of all relevant events and any changes in her plans. This process is often referred to as 'consultation' – particularly where it involves a decision that will fundamentally affect a child, such as a change in foster placement. If, after this exchange of views and information, the local authority remain convinced that a particular route will be in the child's best interests, they have an obligation to pursue it even if the guardian disagrees. Where there are significant disagreements, it may be necessary to return to court to put the matter before the magistrates or the judge. Although guardians are powerful figures in the court setting, the local authority social worker should not feel intimidated but, as a representative of the local authority, should have the support of others in the agency.

Like any working relationship, local authority social workers and guardians need to treat each other with consideration and respect. Good communication at all times is at the heart of a relationship that works in the interests of the child. The context of a highly stressful decision-making process in the courts – and the inevitable anxiety arising from the sense of responsibility that both guardians and social workers feel for the outcome for the child – should not be allowed to affect the professionalism of either guardians or social workers.

Conclusion

The task of supporting children through court proceedings where their future is to be decided is never an easy one for social workers. It is a matter of living with one's own anxiety and the uncertainty about the outcome while providing a reliable and consistent source of support for the child, who is trying to cope with her personal anxiety. When hearings are delayed or resources, such as the 'right' foster home, are not yet available, it is especially difficult to visit the child – and perhaps tempting to postpone the visit to a time of greater certainty. It is at those times that the child will need the social worker most.

Further reading

Pizzey, S. and Davis, J. (1995) *A Guide for Guardians ad Litem in Public Law Proceedings under the Children Act 1989* (London: HMSO).
This book sets out guidance for guardians, but it also contains clarification of the guardian's role that would be of interest to social workers. It covers issues around expert evidence and includes references to judgements made since the implementation of the Children Act that have clarified points of law and set precedents.

Schofield, G. and Thoburn, J. (1996) *Child Protection: The Voice of the Child in Decision Making* (London:Institute of Public Policy Research).
Schofield and Thoburn were commissioned by the Institute for Public Policy Research to examine the research and the issues involved in children's participation in decision-making, in both the child protection system and the courts.

Selwyn, J. (1996) Ascertaining children's wishes and feelings in relation to adoption, *Adoption and Fostering*, **20**, pp. 14–20.
Research on the extent to which children's views are ascertained during the adoption process.

6

Children Looked After by the Local Authority

Introduction

Social work with children looked after by the local authority draws on skills and values shared with other areas of social work practice with children, but there are some important and distinctive aspects of practice that social workers need to develop. However, these are rarely seen as specific skills. Social workers involved in child protection investigations or taking cases to court generally receive specialised training. Social workers who are responsible for children in foster or residential care often get less help in defining what constitutes good practice in relation to their face-to-face work with the child. Where children are placed with carers who are meeting their everyday needs, the nature of an appropriate relationship between worker and child may seem hard to define. Are social workers to be mere representatives of the social services bureaucracy or do they have the opportunity to play a much more significant part in the child's life? This chapter will begin by looking at the context of this work and then look in some detail at models of good practice in face-to-face work with the child.

Legal framework

Children who are looked after by the local authority fall broadly into two legal categories:

- *Children who are accommodated (s.20).* These are either children whose parents are unable to care for them and have actively requested that the child is looked after, or children whose parents have agreed with the local authority, after discussions, that it would safeguard or promote the child's welfare to be looked after by the local authority. Accommodation of children only occurs with the agreement of the parents unless the child is over the age of 16 and can agree on her own behalf.

- *Children who are subject to a Care Order (s.31).* When a Care Order is made, the local authority is given parental responsibility, shared with the parent, for a child until the child reaches the age of 18. There are also obligations concerning the welfare of the care leaver until the age of 21(s.24).

The figures suggest that slightly more than half of the 48,800 children looked after in 1994 were the subject of Care Orders (Department of Health 1996a). In both legal categories, the parents continue to have parental responsibility, only losing it in the event of an Adoption Order being made. Where a Care Order is in force, parental responsibility is shared with the local authority, which has the right to limit the exercise by the parents of their parental responsibility. Although there is a difference in the legal status of the child, a child with a similar problem might be looked after under either legislative provision depending on the circumstances of the child and the circumstances of the parents. The work of the social worker with the child is likely to be affected to varying degrees by the difference in legal status and the differences in parental responsibility. What these situations have in common, however, is the need for the social worker to negotiate between birth parents, carers and the child when decisions are made, both major decisions about the child's future and lesser decisions about the child's day-to-day care. One dilemma for the social worker is the exercise of power and responsibility for the child on behalf of the local authority, while consulting and sharing in the decision-making process with others. Decisions, such as which adult will accompany a child to a hospital appointment, will need to be carefully discussed with all parties and particularly with the child.

Practice context

Needs of the children

We know that social factors, such as housing and poverty, play a major part in determining which children are looked after by the local authority (Bebbington and Miles 1989). Given that broad context, children may need to be looked after by the local authority because of a range of specific difficulties, for example:

- disability
- parental rejection
- being out of control, including criminal behaviour
- physical, emotional or sexual abuse
- neglect
- childhood psychiatric disorder
- parents with mental illness, substance misuse or learning disability, or in prison.

These children's experiences of childhood, family life, education and the community will have been diverse within a likely environment of poverty and deprivation. Their needs will be equally diverse and it is this which the care system will have to address. Social workers who are looking for supplementary or substitute family or residential care for a child have the responsibility for identifying the specific needs of the child and then matching these with an available resource that they believe can best meet those needs. Working with the child to define needs is an essential part of the process. Even with babies and very young children, time spent with the child can enable the social worker to get a clearer sense of the child's perspective, the child's attachments and the child's capacity to cope with change.

Systems for planning and reviewing the placement of children

There has been extensive research into the routes of children through the care system, for example, as summarised in *Patterns and Outcomes in Child Placement* (Department of Health 1991a) and Thoburn (1994). All social workers need to familiarise themselves with research on planning and placement. Much of the pressure to ensure that the choice of option meets the needs of the child started in the 1970s with research that raised concerns about the possibility of 'drift' in care (Rowe and Lambert 1973) but has persisted as difficulties continue to arise in ensuring that good decisions are made for children. This, together with a wish to ensure the quality of a child's experience of care, led to an increased emphasis in the Children Act 1989 on planning and monitoring children in the looked-after system.

After the implementation of the Children Act 1989, the Department of Health, in collaboration with a number of experts in the field, brought out a radical new and detailed system for assessment and planning for children, called 'Looking After Children' (1991). This system is designed to ensure that children have good outcomes and receive a high standard of parental care that meets their needs at each age and stage. The system seems likely to have a major impact on looked-after children, on those involved as carers for children and on social workers for children. It has been widely adopted by social services departments and is also being developed by a number of foreign countries for use in ensuring high standards in the care of children. It consists of a structure and materials for planning for children and for assessing and reviewing outcomes. The welfare of children is looked at along seven dimensions:

- health
- education
- identity
- family and social relationships
- social presentation
- emotional and behavioural development
- self-care skills.

The documents themselves ask for detailed information, relevant to each age group and specific to each child. Each action and assessment record, for example, will require answers to questions that cover the full range of activities under each dimension. The care plans and assessment and action records are extremely useful in establishing how the child is developing at any point in time on each dimension, identifying who will take responsibility for improving outcomes for the child and revising plans accordingly. In addition, the process of responding to the answers to the questions asked by the forms should ensure that all those who have some responsibility for the child will be involved. Perhaps most importantly, the expectation is that the child will be as fully involved as possible in compiling the information and contributing her own ideas, wishes and feelings. This participation in the process will, for many children, include attending review and planning meetings and will for all children include clear messages about the ways in which their views have been communicated to meetings and taken into account.

Working with birth families

Supporting the birth family and maintaining children's links with their birth family will be a key responsibility of the social worker. Research has demonstrated that, in most cases, contact between children and their birth families will contribute to the success of a placement (Thoburn 1990; Fratter *et al.* 1991). The social worker will need to help the child to clarify her feelings about contact and be involved, as well as the parents, in deciding on the arrangements so that contact can be 'comfortable' for all parties (Thoburn 1994). Children need to feel relaxed and they need to feel safe. In a national survey (Fletcher 1993), the majority (70 per cent) of looked-after children felt that they had the right amount of contact, but many would have liked the arrangements for contact to be different.

Not unconnected with the important issue of contact is the fact that 87 per cent of children who are looked after by local authorities return at some point to live with their families (Bullock *et al.* 1993). The message must be that, however successful the systems for care and accommodation in looking after children, birth families continue to play an important role for the vast majority of children. Any model of social work practice with children looked after must take that into account. As ever, though, listening to the child and understanding their feelings about birth families continues to be important.

What children in foster and residential care say about their social workers

The views of looked after children about their social workers are particularly helpful in developing models of good practice. Fletcher (1993) summarised the responses to a questionnaire that was sent to children in foster and residential care with the publication *Who Cares?* The overwhelming majority of children said positive things about their social workers. Some of them described personal qualities that clearly mattered, such as being 'funny', 'friendly', 'nice', 'considerate, a good person' (p. 18).

There were still a wide range of comments from individual children, some suggesting the important role the social worker played in their lives, others expressing anger or disappointment at not being understood:

> She is like a very best friend. (Eleven year old, foster care)

You need a social worker in care. They're brilliant. (Thirteen year old residential care)

I think my social worker should be sacked.

I don't get on with her and I feel she doesn't understand me (Sixteen year old, residential care). (p. 21)

Although the majority of children reported that they felt listened to about changes in their lives and moves of placement, many expressed concerns about the way in which decisions were made and the extent to which their views were taken into account in practice.

The report concluded that by far the highest number of respondents described the good things about their social workers in terms of their relationship with them and focused on the social worker's ability to enable them to talk about their feelings and to listen. These core skills in communicating, listening and relationship-building will be major themes as we look at the nature of the social worker's work with the child.

For many children, the social worker's capacity to listen needed also to be linked with action. In research conducted by the NSPCC, one 11-year-old said:

The good ones have been kind to me. They do things quickly once they say they'll do something. They understand how you act and what's on your mind...

(The others?)

Oh. they never get things done, they're always making promises they never keep. (Butler and Williamson 1994:99)

Getting things done in a way that matches the child's timescale may not be easy. Some of those things, such as finding a foster home, may be outside the social worker's control. Maintaining a constructive and trusting relationship with a child in those circumstances needs additional work, including attentive listening to the child and openness about the realities of the situation.

Principles for face-to-face work

The face-to-face work of the social worker with the child will need to reflect traditional core skills and values such as genuineness, warmth and empathy, and the ability to treat the child with respect. Whether the plan is for the child to return home in the near future or the placement is likely to be permanent, certain principles will be helpful in defining good practice:

- *Respect.* The social worker should demonstrate respect for the child as an individual, taking account of the needs of the child relating to age, race, religion, gender, sexual orientation or disability.
- *Relationship.* The worker and child need to build warmth and trust within the professional relationship.
- *Privacy.* It is important to see the child on her own, in an environment where she feels comfortable.
- *Confidentiality.* From the beginning, it is essential to define the boundaries of confidentiality, explaining protection issues and agency requirements.
- *Reliability.* Developing a relationship of trust requires a social worker to be on time, to do what she said she would or to explain why she was not able to.
- *Availability.* Although a social worker cannot be available at all hours, it is necessary to ensure that the child knows how to reach her social worker and that the worker responds promptly.
- *Honest and open communication.* A social worker must keep the child informed about any proposed changes or plans affecting the child. Be open when there are problems.
- *Participation.* It is the child's right to be and to feel involved. The social worker can enable the child to contribute her views when decisions are made, in whatever way the child feels comfortable. This will mean using materials that are consistent with the child's race, gender, age and understanding.
- *Partiality.* It is important to make the child feel special and important to the social worker as an individual: not just remembering birthdays, but remembering the favourite chocolate bar or football team. Small things give powerful messages about continuity and caring.
- *Respect for the child's birth family.* Whatever the circumstances, the social worker should demonstrate respect and concern for the child's birth family.

- *Respect for carers.* However the relationship between the worker and the child develops, it is essential to demonstrate respect for foster carers or residential staff.

In addition to these core principles, there are some distinctive characteristics of the social worker's face-to-face work with the child in the care system that need special attention. Three major and connected themes provide a way of clarifying these issues. The first is the theme of attachment, separation and loss. Whatever the circumstances of the child's separation from her family, these will be relevant. The second is the child's need to make sense of the past, in both a cognitive and emotional way. Finally, there is the work to be done to facilitate the child's participation in decision-making. Children will only be able to exercise their right to participate if they have been able to clarify their feelings and ideas about their situation and have the fullest possible information about decision-making processes and available options.

Attachment, separation and loss

Children's attachments and close relationships contribute to all aspects of a child's development (see Chapter 2). Children looked after by the local authority will all have experienced separation and loss, whether the child is in temporary respite care for a matter of weeks during a family crisis or permanently separated following abuse or family breakdown (Fahlberg 1994). The child who is looked after may be aware of certain gains, particularly if her experiences of family life have been very stressful or abusive. However, for most children, the experience of loss following separation may bear many of the emotional, cognitive and behavioural characteristics of a bereavement. As a starting point, it is therefore useful to consider the stages of reaction to loss that have been associated with bereavement and the impact of these on the child with whom one is working:

- shock/denial
- searching
- anger/blame
- sadness/despair
- understanding and acceptance
- integration.

These stages are set out in relation to children in a number of key texts (for example Aldgate and Simmonds 1988; Fahlberg 1994; Jewett 1994). It is important for the social worker to be aware of the manifestations of grief and loss in looked-after children. In particular, the social worker needs to interpret correctly disturbed behaviours that are a reaction to loss so that they are not incorrectly interpreted either as evidence that the child is unhappy in that foster or residential placement or perhaps as evidence of previous parental neglect or abuse.

Factors affecting the experience of separation: implications for practice

The stages of grief do not represent a rigid process through which children will go regardless of circumstances. Certain children, like adults, may move at a different pace or may get stuck at a different stage. There are also a number of other factors that will affect the way in which children looked after will react to separation when in foster or residential care.

Loss of attachment figures

Children with secure attachments who are separated from their attachment figures are likely to be overwhelmed with anxiety because they no longer have access to a secure base. Children who have insecure attachments to their parents, as is quite likely for children who have experienced extreme adversity necessitating their move into foster or residential care, may find it even more difficult to build a relationship with the substitute carer. They may not have an inner working model of relationships that inclines them to build trust in adults (Bowlby 1980). All children, whatever the quality of their previous attachments, are likely to experience a natural sense of belonging and shared identity with family members, which is threatened by the separation. As Aldgate has suggested:

> intervention designed to effect mediation of the negative effects of separation and loss must be based on a fundamental belief that separation involves fear which needs to be mastered, and that loss involves grief which needs to be expressed. (Aldgate, 1988:44)

The expression of feelings in relation to separation is also important in the context of building new attachments with substitute carers.

Adversity, abuse and ambivalence

Children who have experienced multiple adversities, such as domestic violence or abuse, are likely to have impaired coping strategies. Children recently accommodated may be coming to terms with their past experience of serious family problems or rejection, while grieving about the current separation and perhaps missing siblings, other family members or family pets. Here the experience of ambivalence will be central. Even for children who have experienced quite serious forms of abuse or neglect, very few experience a sense of relief at being safe which is not in some way mixed with sadness about the loss of family members and concern for their welfare. The nature of their experiences within their families will affect their view of the separation. The following case examples illustrate how both abusive experiences and varied patterns of relationships affect the nature of the loss.

CASE STUDY

Sally, a 13-year-old black girl, had been beaten and sexually abused over a number of years by her stepfather. She had been too frightened to tell anyone. Although she was greatly relieved to be safe in foster care, she missed her younger half-brother who was still at home and felt guilty about involving social workers in the family. She suffered anxiety about the welfare of her brother, who had also been physically abused.

CASE STUDY

Donna, a nine year old girl, had been neglected because of her mother's serious alcohol problem. Donna had spent many brief spells in foster care when her mother couldn't care for her and she had witnessed domestic violence. Finally she said that she wanted to stay with foster carers until her Mum stopped drinking. She felt very anxious about her mother and needed to see her regularly to check if she was all right. (Schofield 1996:152)

In different ways, children bring with them aspects of their past, be it disturbed behaviour or feelings of anxiety and guilt. Reactions to loss must be worked with in that context.

Helping the child cope with moves

Children who have experienced multiple separations are likely to have little sense of control of their destiny, and a state of learned helplessness (Seligman 1975) may develop. Both adversity and loss sensitise children to further losses. Children develop a cognitive set that affects their reactions to stresses and increases their vulnerability.

Awareness of such issues around separation and loss should enable the social worker to help the child at times of moves – either from one placement to another or from placement to home. A great deal of attention has been paid to aspects of preparing children for permanent placement, particularly in the form of life-story work, which will be addressed later in the chapter. However, many more children are changing placements or returning home than move into adoption, and there is a great deal of evidence that the service provided is not comparable. Given that even children who return home are often returning to a changed household (Bullock *et al.* 1993), all these children should be deemed to be in need not only of preparation, but also support during the transition and afterwards in the new home, whether with birth families or substitute carers. It is essential to offer the same degree of help to the child, as well as to the new carers or parents, to resolve anxieties about separation and to enable the new placement to cope with the child's feelings. (See also Smith 1994 for an account of the attachment difficulties that lead to disruptions.)

Loss of the familiar

When children are placed in foster or residential care, they can find this change of environment very stressful. They may worry that that their old home and their old life has simply disappeared. As well as the sense of loss of the old, there are difficulties in adjusting to the new and the unfamiliar, both the environment and the way of doing things. The age and developmental stage of the child will affect this process. Babies will be very sensitive to changes in the view from the cot, and sounds and smells will be different. Young children who are just able to walk round the furniture at home become disorientated by a completely different set of furniture. Children who are just becoming more able to be independent by getting their own breakfast find themselves in a strange kitchen where nothing seems to be in the right place. Teenagers find that it threatens their new-found sense of identity to be away from the bedroom that has been carefully covered with things reflecting that identity. Children in placement need a great deal of extra help to feel comfortable with the new environment and to learn the informal rules of the new home. If they can get a sense of control in their lives, they can begin to master their feelings about the separation. Social workers have a dual role to play – direct support to the child and support to the carers in permitting and surviving the expression of powerful feelings.

Race and culture

Children from minority ethnic or religious groups may be placed in an environment that is quite alien to them. The debate about the need for same-race placements has highlighted this issue but clearly, whatever the long-term outcome, children in a placement that does not reflect their own ethnic or cultural background are subjected to additional losses and greater challenges are involved in coming to terms with separation from family and friends. Social workers as well as carers need to think carefully about how they acknowledge these core dilemmas for children. One child felt that the system had failed him:

> They never sat me down and asked how I was feeling… I felt frustrated. How could they deny me my race, my identity, who I am? (Jones and Butt 1995:81)

However, some care needs to be taken about making assumptions based on a superficial assessment of needs, and a child still wants to be seen as an individual with her own views. An Asian girl who was given an Asian social worker complained about the pressure she was put under:

> Why aren't you a good Muslim Girl, put Indian clothes on… I prefer my jeans and trainers. (Butler and Williamson 1994:103)

Disability

Children with physical or learning disabilities are more vulnerable in all situations, including coping with the consequences of separation. A lack of understanding of the reason for the separation can cause extra distress, as can self-blame associated with the disability. One 10-year-old girl with a physical disability commented that her mother would not have neglected and rejected her had her legs worked properly.

Social workers may need to gain the assistance of experts in different aspects of disability in order to offer sensitive and appropriate help.

Leaving care

One of the most difficult moves or separations involves teenagers who are leaving care after a period in foster or residential care. These young people are likely to be vulnerable in a number of ways, yet are expected to separate from carers and achieve 'independence' at an earlier age than other young people – often at 16 or 17 years old rather than in their 20s. The transition from care to independence has been very well documented by Stein and his colleagues, and all social workers need to familiarise themselves with their research (Stein and Carey 1986; Biehal *et al.* 1995). Their findings suggest that, in addition to the practical help that young people need, there is a need for a sense of continuity with significant people in their lives, who may be family members, foster carers or social workers. Specialist leaving-care teams will have an important role to play for many young people, but social workers also have a place in helping young people through this transition, both by maintaining a relationship with young people and by helping them to sustain links with family members. Where workers have known a young person during her childhood, they can act as a bridge to independence or, in most cases, have a continuing role in facilitating 'interdependence'.

Making sense of the past and the present

When we start to think about the child's efforts to understand and come to terms with her sense of loss over time and to build new relationships, we need to understand the importance of making sense of events for the child's long-term development and particularly for the child's emotional health. This process is a priority if the child is to be able to move on psychologically, emotionally or practically in terms of a successful return home or move to a new family. It is in this area that the links between cognitive and emotional factors are at their strongest. We know from the context of attachment theory and the development of self-esteem and identity that the predictability and continuity of close relationships enables the child to move forward developmentally. Where the child's life has been disrupted, the child can become stuck at certain stages. Alternatively, the child may construct a version of her childhood that may be based on a mix of misunderstanding, self-blame, fantasy, magical thinking and defensive attempts to protect her own self-esteem. The child appears to move on, but behaviours may become self-destructive or antisocial as these attempts to make sense of the past fail to reflect reality or perpetuate poor self-esteem.

Fahlberg (1994) has suggested that there are a number of ways in which children make sense of this separation and that each explanation has consequences for children's view of their situation and their emotional reaction to it:

- Children may think that they have been *taken away* from their parents or kidnapped. This threatens their sense of confidence in their parents' power to protect them and leads to *heightened anxiety*.

- Children may fear that they have been *given away* by their parents. This means that they were not good enough and leads to *sadness and depression*.

- Children may believe that *they have caused* the loss of the parent by something they have done. This may lead to the child feeling excessively *powerful and responsible* for subsequent events.

Getting in touch with the child's reality

When the child is able to trust the worker, the child may wish to express her feelings and ideas through drawings or play. The use of structured materials such as an ecomap (Fahlberg 1994) may allow children to place themselves clearly in a practical sense in relation to significant others (Figure 6.1). It is often easier to start with the practical in the here and now, who is in the family and living where, which school, name of foster carers and so on, before inviting children to express their feelings about their situation.

Children may need to talk about their feelings of anger – often directed towards the foster carer or the social worker rather than towards the parents. This is a very natural process, and the child needs to be listened to without contradiction. Defensiveness is not helpful. If children feel that their feelings have been listened to, they will in time feel safe enough to find their own way of expressing their feelings of sadness or anger. However, in the first instance, the goal is to build a relationship of trust, which can only develop if children feel that their ideas and feelings are being taken seriously.

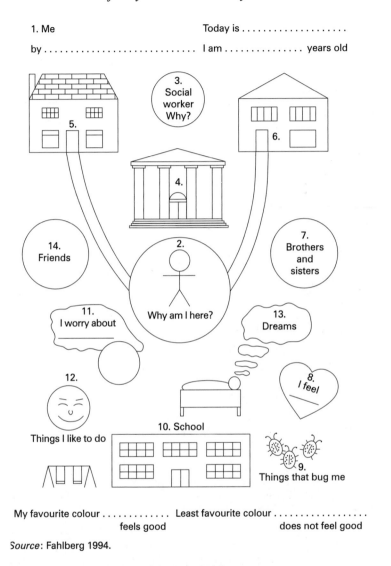

Figure 6.1   Child's Ecomap

Similarly, the child's anxieties about the reasons for being looked after need to be heard and not instantly contradicted. For example, when the child says, 'My parents rejected me because I'm stupid and ugly', it is important to resist the temptation to immediately jump in with a comment such as 'Oh surely not, you're very clever and pretty' but instead to ask, 'What makes you think that?' Reassuring the child may make the worker feel better – it may even temporarily make the child feel better – but in the context of the work, it gives the child the message that the worker's reality is more important than the child's and she may not trust the social worker with her fears again.

Working at the child's pace

For some children, attempts at talking about events or feelings and using materials in a structured way may be almost impossible in the early days of a placement. Their behaviour may be too distractible and wild, either because this behaviour was a feature of their disturbance before coming into care or because it is a reaction to anxiety about the separation. Other, simple, factors in relationship-building will then prove very important, such as making regular visits at times the child knows about and setting aside time to spend with the child, even if this is time spent reading a story or playing. This more informal time can be a preliminary or addition to more focused work; it should not be a substitute for giving the child opportunities to explore her feelings unless the worker is satisfied that the child is able to do this with the carers.

The process of life-story work

Making sense of the past is too often seen as relating to a particular point in time when a life-story book is produced. Although this is a useful and for many children an essential item, it should only form one part of a continuous process of enabling children to understand and reflect on their past and present. Similarly, because this process is so important for children, we need to be aware of its usefulness, not only for children in long term substitute care, but also for those who are looked after for briefer periods. For children who have had very disrupted early lives, perhaps moving around a great deal within the birth family, experiencing significant losses or facing significant family adversities, the period in accommodation may provide a valuable opportunity for the social worker to work with the child to sort out her ideas and feelings. This can in itself be seen as an important piece of preventive child care work. Again, it is important to learn lessons from permanent placement skills, which can be readily applied to help the vast majority of looked-after children – the children who go home.

The child's right to her history

Children need not only to express feelings about the past and the present, but also to build a picture for themselves of the pattern of events that has led to their separation from parents and the events that have subsequently occurred. For children who grow up in their birth families, family history is retained through the everyday process of reminiscing about past events and family members. For children in care or accommodation, this process has been interrupted and, for many, it is necessary to construct what in many ways is an artificial means of enabling the child to hang onto her history. One element of this process is to ensure that, from the earliest stages, detailed records are kept of family members and significant events in the child's life. Research has shown that, too often in the past, when children have been separated from their families, it later becomes almost impossible for the young person to have a complete account of her origins or to rebuild family links (Harrison and Mason 1994).

Making connections

Children need to be able to make the connections in their past, both factually – for example, why did the social worker change at that point? why had there to be a change of school? – and emotionally – why did my mother stop coming to visit? why did those foster carers change their mind about adopting me? what does this mean about the kind of person I am? This process helps to clarify the children's ideas about themselves but, very importantly, encourages them to feel that events are not random, that life has patterns that can be understood and explained. What you do today is remembered and *does* have an effect tomorrow. People to whom you were once important do not forget you just because they are no longer in touch. The past has value in the present.

Once is never enough

Discussions with the child about the past may need to be held at a particular point in time, this timing often being determined by external factors such as a change of placement. The child may be ready for this kind of work at any stage, and facts and feelings will need to be returned to at intervals. The developmental stage of the child will dictate the kinds of explanation and the language that is used. As the child remains longer in placement, or perhaps returns to the birth family, there will be more changes and events to fit into the picture. However, there will also be a need to revisit previous areas of information dealt with when the child was younger, so that the questions that the older child asks can be answered.

Encourage the child to own the work

The worker should fully involve the child in planning the process of the work, not only in sharing ideas and feelings, but also in matters such as discussing whether to do a family tree or a genogram, whether to use different colour felt tips or whether to do the work in the living room or at the office. At every stage, the worker should allow the child to say what particular drawings or photographs mean to her. The worker's comments should be tentative and aimed at enabling the child to clarify her own ideas and feelings rather than offering clever interpretations to which the child might find it hard to say no. Children in care or accommodation may have had numerous professional adults try to assess them and make sense of them, and write very public reports about them. It is important in this work to ensure that the child feels able to regain some personal ownership of her life history.

Quality of the child/worker relationship

The child's capacity or readiness to engage in this work will depend entirely on the quality of the work with the child already undertaken and the quality of the relationship with the worker. The work with the senses (Oaklander 1978), the work to explore feelings around separation and loss, the building of a relationship of trust with the worker – all precede the detailed exploration of facts and feelings about the past and the present. For this reason, it is important that, wherever possible, the work throughout the process is undertaken by the same person. Too often a child has developed a close relationship with a particular social worker during a difficult time at home, perhaps court proceedings, perhaps several moves of foster home, and then life-story work is given to a different worker, perhaps a student, because it is seen as a time-consuming but discrete piece of work. If the social worker feels she lacks specific skills, she should have consultation or supervision from more specialist workers for the duration of certain pieces of more difficult work. This is a much better use of the specialist worker's skills and protects the child's relationship with the worker.

Life-story books

One basic issue that needs to be established at the beginning of such a project is who the work and the book are for. If the book is purely for the benefit of the child in an emotional sense or to keep as a record, it should not be part of a formal assessment. However, there may still be issues of confidentiality. Will information be shared in other forums, such as reviews? Who will decide this? Who will keep the book after it is complete: the child or the substitute carers? If the child is to have some sense of ownership of the work and the product, in the form of a book, this must be discussed at the beginning.

Life-story work can include the following:

- *Where I came from.* The place of birth, birth weight, birth certificate, baby photographs, especially of being held in a parent's arms, are all powerful triggers for children. At that stage, they were totally dependent and, being newborn, could not be deemed to be anything other than a 'good' baby with parents who had yet to be anything other than totally caring. Again, the process of establishing this important context for the child is important. Sometimes unexpected family connections can be unearthed. The father of a 10-year-old boy who had lost touch with his son soon after the birth was traced by a social worker. It transpired that the boy had been born prematurely and been in the special care unit after birth, and that the father had kept in his wallet a photograph of his son in his special care cot. Although the photograph itself was significant, much more significant for the child was the fact that his father had carried it all those years. This information becomes part of the written account of the child's life but more importantly stays in the child's memory and contributes to his sense of his own worth.

- *Life path.* Building on the 'where did I come from?' might be a life path that simply sets out the dates, main events and perhaps feelings at each stage. This can be done in words or children might like to choose colours or use drawings to denote certain stages in their history, certain foster homes, for example, or friends.

- *Family tree.* Family trees help the child to get a fuller picture of family relationships. For some children, drawing a simple tree with names on to get a sense of who is in the birth family can lead to something more like a geneogram. Several trees, or trees with several branches, may be needed for children who have had a number of significant families in their lives, including substitute families. It is important to remember that, even for adults, the process of drawing out family connections, noting births, deaths, marriages and separations, noting which households certain adults and children now live in, is very powerful. Children may start to see patterns, again as adults do. They may be brought face to face with the fact that their mother separated from all her male children once they reached teenage years, or that all their brothers and sisters are spread out in different families or foster homes. They may fear that there is an inevitability about patterns of behaviour over the generations. One 15-year-old girl who had been sexually abused by her mother's partners found this easier to come to terms with when she realised that her own mother had been abused as a child. However, she said that she did not want children herself because the same thing would happen to them. This fear needed to be a focus of future work. The difficulty of working with children in this area is the mix of fact, fantasy and feeling. Children's ideas and feelings about family relationships need to be listened to. Facts that contradict the child's previously held beliefs must be gently introduced, particularly if the information is painful. It is better to have the true story, carefully explained, than a fantasy, which may have to be corrected in adolescence or in adult life when less support is available.

- *Photographs of significant people and places.* Part of the background work that the social worker will need to do is to assemble photographs of places where the child has lived or gone to school, or of people who may be significant. This can involve quite considerable amounts of detective work, writing to previous foster carers or family members to see what can be found that the child will find helpful. It is especially important to involve the child in the process. Are there people that the child remembers? Was there a family pet who mattered? It is worth having an extra set of these photographs for the child's file so that, in later life, this forms a record that can be turned to if the book has been lost or destroyed.

- *Visiting people and places from the past.* For some children, there will be a number of places that they remember or perhaps lived in when they were very young. It may be possible for the child to be taken to visit people or places. Once again, the powerful impact of such visits on children means that they should be carefully prepared. People being visited need also to be carefully prepared, and all parties need the opportunity to debrief afterwards, in case there is unfinished business that may stay with the adults or child in an unhelpful way into the future. Equally, for these visits, the child needs to be accompanied by the worker whom the child trusts and who knows the child well enough to see when she is getting anxious or may need help.

- *Memory box.* This is an idea developed at Barnardos Positive Options to help children whose parents suffer from HIV/Aids to collect and preserve items that can provide memories. These may be soft toys or a picture, a dried flower or an audio or video cassette. Children in care or accommodation have often lost things as well as people, but there may be some things which a child has that can be preserved. It may also be possible to start a box with things currently that matter, giving the message that things are worth remembering and can last.

- *Life story.* Children will need help in putting their story together, and this is often done as a piece of continuous prose, either linking photographs or other items, or on its own. This can be written in the first person, second person or third person, depending on which seems appropriate. For the baby, it may be appropriate for the birth parent or the social worker to write a letter for later life, which contains information about the birth family and an explanation of why the child was placed in a substitute family. Each child's life story will be very different in the way in which it is written – the age of the child alone will dictate the kind of language and concepts that may be used. There is no easy answer to the fact that what is written to be read to a 4-year-old may seem rather inappropriate when the child is much older. However, children can understand the context of the writing and, as long as the current questions of the older child can be answered, this should not be a problem. Many older children would get a stronger sense of their 4-year-old self from such a book, and this could itself be helpful for them.

What do children do with their life-story books? Some hold onto them; others leave them in the care of their carers as a rather special object. Hopefully, children will be given strong messages that they can look at it whenever they want to. Children may still be anxious about whether such a request would upset the new family, so it would seem to be desirable to bring the book out at intervals, particularly at key points in family life. Perhaps when there is a new baby or grandchild in the foster family, it might be interesting for the child to look at the photograph of herself as a baby. The book is once again a means to an end – to enable the child to talk about feelings, putting them into words, rather than avoiding, repressing them or acting them out.

Some life-story books can have an important role even when they appear to have been forgotten.

CASE STUDY

Peter was 9 years old and was to be adopted by the foster carers with whom he had lived for 6 years. When the new social worker went to visit, she asked the foster carers whether Peter had a life-story book. They said he had but he never looked at it and never mentioned his birth family, with whom there was no contact. When the social worker saw Peter on his own and asked about his family, he immediately rummaged in the back of the wardrobe and came up with a life-story book that was rather brief and seemed to be falling apart. Nevertheless, it had photographs of Peter as a baby and with his mother and two brothers. He dwelled on the photograph of his mother and said he wondered what she looked like now. The social worker, who had met the mother, was able to reassure him that his mother was well and still had Peter's photograph up on the wall in her living room. These conversations led to further discussions with the adoptive parents and the mother, resulting in contact being renewed.

Participation in decision-making

Throughout this chapter, there has been an emphasis on helping children and young people to resolve feelings and gain knowledge and understanding. Part of this work is a commitment to enabling the child to develop a positive sense of self-worth and a sense of being an actor in his own life rather than just a passive recipient of 'care'. Involving children in decision-making is another direct and specific area that social workers need to address if they wish to ensure that children feel that their voices matter.

Children and young people in substitute care face a situation in which a number of adults may have legal responsibility for them (parents, local authorities, social workers), day-to-day care of them (foster carers, residential carers, family members) or other significant relationships with them (older siblings, grandparents, teachers). Decision-making is inevitably a complex process, whether on major issues such as a change of placement or on more minor, but nevertheless important, issues from the child's point of view, such as clothes or food. The reviewing systems for children looked after described above require the involvement of children when decisions are made, and many children will wish to attend meetings or communicate their views in more indirect ways to those who are part of this network of adults. They will, of course, require help, not only from the individual social worker, but also from the carers, parents and others who have a role to play in the review process. A culture of respect for young people's views and feelings needs to be consciously created. Feedback from young people in the care system consistently reports that the majority feel at meetings that they have been ignored or that their views have been listened to but not taken seriously (Fletcher 1993).

In addition to these more formal and procedural decision-making processes, it is the responsibility of the key worker to ensure that children have an ongoing route for communicating their wishes and feelings. Being asked their opinion about a proposed decision places children in a passive role. There may be issues that they wish to raise about a problem in their lives of which adults are unaware. If there are problems of bullying at school, for example, the child may be unclear as to whether this an issue to be dealt with by the foster carer or the social worker, handled within the school itself or mentioned to the birth parent at the next visit. Children's capacity to express themselves and be active in bringing issues to the attention of relevant adults will vary enormously and knowing who to go to will be only a part of the picture. Young children or children who have a disability, particularly those who have mobility or communication problems, will need additional assistance. Each child or young person will need their own routes to those who can help them to have a voice. This may be through the social worker but it may be through an independent visitor, appointed when looked-after children have no regular visitor, an advocate or simply the parent of a friend at school.

Participation in decision-making by children, in this arena as in others, will not mean handing over total responsibility for the decision to the child or young person, any more than children growing up in their birth families are given total control. However, increasingly the young person needs to be allowed to take more responsibility and more risks in order to learn how to cope with a degree of autonomy. This is a natural part of good parenting. Children who leave care have, in some cases, been given too little autonomy and find that these are very difficult lessons to learn in later years at a time when they are losing other supports (Biehal *et al.* 1995).

Social workers need to be sure that, in addition to other mechanisms for participation, children have knowledge about and access to a complaints procedures. All local authorities are required to have proper complaints procedures for children who receive their services, and many have developed specific information leaflets for those in their care. Giving children such leaflets is a strong message that children have the legal right to expect a certain quality of care and, if they are worried about what is happening to them, they are entitled to voice their concern and have a proper response.

Conclusion

Children who are looked after by the local authority need to be able to rely on their social worker not just to make practical arrangements, locate substitute carers, arrange contact or set up review meetings. They also need a commitment that the social worker will be consistently and reliably concerned about the child's welfare, will be sensitive to the child's needs and will be available to listen to the child. The specific areas of work around separation and loss, life-story books or participation are strands of what should be a coherent relationship, in which the child knows where he stands and can develop trust. The social worker is unlikely to be the most important adult in the child's life on a day-to-day basis, as this is more likely to be a foster or residential carer. However, it is essential not to underestimate how important the continuous and reliable relationship with a trusted social worker can be for many troubled children.

Further reading

Fahlberg, V. (1994) *A Child's Journey Through Placement* (London: BAAF).
Vera Fahlberg is an American child psychotherapist who has worked extensively with children in placement. This book is an essential text for those who want to understand the connections between children's development, particularly attachments and behaviour patterns, and family placement. It also gives ideas for social work practitioners to help them help children through each stage.

Jewett, C. (1994) *Helping Children Cope with Separation and Loss,* 2nd edn (London: Batsford/BAAF).

This is a classic text for practitioners wishing to learn how to work effectively with children who have experienced separation and loss. Although not exclusively about children in substitute care, it will prepare social workers to understand and work more sensitively with such children.

Ryan, T. and Walker, R. (1993) *Life Story Work* (London: BAAF).

This is a very practical guide for those wishing to undertake life-story work. It needs to be read in the context of the other texts, which provide the psychological context for the work.

Thoburn, J. (1994) *Child Placement: Principles and Practice,* 2nd edn * (Aldershot: Arena).

Thoburn is a distinguished child care researcher and here she makes important links between research findings and practice in child placement. The book offers guidance to social workers about how to plan for, as well as work with, children looked after by local authorities.

7

Children and Youth Justice

by Nigel Stone

Introduction

Prominently placed over the main entrance to the Central Criminal Court at the Old Bailey, an edict in stone exhorts us to 'Defend the children of the poor and punish the wrongdoer'. In practice, rather more energy is devoted to castigating children's wrongdoings and extending the range of penalties to deal with them. The pre-eminent crime problem is 'teenage lawlessness'; the archetypal problematic offender is the 'rampant', even feral, young lower social class male. Some children have attracted such personal notoriety that they have acquired contemporary folk devil status as 'spiderboy', 'ratboy' and 'safari boy'. This preoccupation is reflected in criminological theory and research. As Coleman and Moynihan (1996:92) remark:

> We could be forgiven for thinking that the whole criminological enterprise has been built mainly upon the activities of young people.

Youth has long attracted respectable fears and moral panics about the threat it is seen to pose to society (Pearson 1983). Brown's (1995) study of adult perceptions of crime in East Middlesborough nicely identifies how adult insecurity and powerlessness, in the face of adverse social change and a decreasing quality of life, are translated into a preoccupation with 'getting young people off the streets'. Other commentators (for example Ferguson 1996) have identified our enduring confusion about our children, increasingly frightened for them because of the dangers they face, and of them because of their apparent lack of obvious stake in the social order.

In contrast, evidence is beginning to accumulate of the true extent of social problems experienced by those most entrenched in the juvenile justice system, helping to challenge the populist folk devil image of young offenders and place them more firmly within the ambit of services for children in need under the Children Act 1989 s.17. Hagell and Newburn (1994), Stewart *et al.* (1994), Bottoms (1995) and Johnson and Parker (1996) have demonstrated the extent of family disruption, school problems, substance misuse and other indicators of reduced life prospects among persistent young offenders. Further pursuing the predicament of young people on the receiving end of changes in social policy, benefit cutbacks and the rundown of welfare, Carlen's (1996) study of homeless young people identifies how crime can feature in the pursuit of a 'survivalist lifestyle' in the face of rejection, disempowerment and latter-day exile. We are also beginning to understand the full extent of youthful victimisation. Research by Anderson *et al.* (1994) in Edinburgh demonstrated that 11–15-year-olds had to cope with startling levels of property, violent and sexual crime that adults would find intolerable, with little recourse to police or other adults, who were perceived to be indifferent or hostile to their problems. Young people reported that their encounters with authority inclined them to keep the adult world at bay, thus amplifying perceptions that they 'share a deliberately exclusive world in which they reject adult values and adult intervention' (Brown 1995).

Juvenile justice in disarray?

Attaining a juvenile justice system that can deal with such a high-profile workload and fulfil the considerable expectations placed upon it is enormously difficult. Ball (1995) has identified 'the erosion of difference between the treatment of children and adults', united now within the overarching principle of 'just deserts' within the Criminal Justice Act 1991, leaving us with little conceptual basis for a distinctive, separate approach to child offenders. Has the children's court outlived its usefulness, as some United States commentators have suggested, calling for its abolition and reintegration into adult justice?

The Audit Commission (1996) has condemned the youth justice system as a highly refined, expensive and inefficient processing mechanism, dealing largely with relatively minor offending by immature individuals who need to be helped out of offending behaviour. Characterising the youth justice system as 'in disarray', the Labour Party (1996) has recently set out a radical agenda for reform, which will provide the foundation for the Crime and Disorder Bill, anticipated to pass through Parliament in 1998.

As Walgrave (1996) points out, all systems of juvenile justice struggle to 'construct a kind of synthesis or compromise between two basic principles that are very hard to reconcile': on the one hand, a penal response emphasising legality, proportionality and responsibility; on the other, what can be characterised as a developmental response, which doubts how functional penality can be for minors. Walgrave suggests that systems commonly resort to '*mystifications du langage*' to camouflage the irreconcilability of these rationales and that any synthesis of penal law and educative principles tends to compound the drawbacks of both systems. The current system in England and Wales continues to enshrine the so-called 'welfare principle' of the Children and Young Persons Act 1933 s.44(1):

> Every court in dealing with a child or young person who is brought before it, either as an offender or otherwise, shall have regard to the welfare of the child or young person...

No guidance, statutory or otherwise, illuminates how s.44(1) should be interpreted or applied and may appear 'a residual or redundant totem of little or no practical bite and significance' (Ball *et al.* 1995). The Criminal Justice Act 1991 failed to clarify the present purpose of s.44(1) in the light of the Children Act 1989 and in no way attempts to build bridges between the parallel criminal and civil jurisdictions affecting children and their families. For example, although local authorities are required by the 1989 Act to take reasonable steps to reduce the need to bring criminal proceedings against children in their area, to encourage children in their area not to commit criminal offences and to avoid the need for children to be placed in secure accommodation, the 1991 Act does not authorise the youth court to require a local authority to undertake an investigation of a child's circumstances and to consider whether application should be made in the family proceedings court for a Care or Supervision Order (akin to the power available to a family court under the Children Act 1989 s.37).

In the American debate of future options, Krisberg and Austin (1993) have called for the 'reinventing' of juvenile justice, a 'revitalised mission' that locates youth justice as a fully fledged justice enterprise but as part of the 'total adolescent care system'. This chapter can only provide a snapshot of the tensions within the current system and sketch some tentative pointers towards revitalisation and reinvention. As good a starting point as any for social workers, and more helpful than s.44(1) as an alternative legend for the Old Bailey stonework, is provided by Article 40 of the UN Convention, which recognises the right of every child in the youth justice system:

> to be treated in a manner consistent with the promotion of the child's sense of dignity and worth, which reinforces the child's respect for the human rights and fundamental freedoms of others and which takes into account the child's age and the desirability of promoting the child's reintegration and the child's assuming a constructive role in society.

Criminal justice processes are predominantly distancing, legalistic, difficult to follow, denunciatory, degradative and exclusionary in character (Garfinkel 1956). In giving practical meaning to the UN Declaration, the juvenile justice system and the social workers who serve it should seek to maximise reintegrative potential by stressing the following principles and values (drawing partly on Braithwaite and Mugford 1994):

- The offence and the perpetrator should be 'uncoupled' so that the act rather than the actor is labelled as irresponsible or 'profane'.
- The process should bring home to the young perpetrator the impact of her behaviour upon others and should avoid or counteract barriers that can distance young people from their actions or which they can otherwise seize upon to avoid responsibility. 'Techniques of neutralisation' (Sykes and Matza 1957) should be challenged appropriately and shame experienced in a constructive way.
- Offending should be placed in a social context for which others in addition to the young perpetrator share some responsibility.
- Intervention should seek to promote rather than undermine the young person's developmental needs.
- Every effort should be made to achieve consensus in achieving 'purposeful endings' that can heal the harm caused by the offending, harness family and community strengths and enhance informal control potential, following up undertakings to ensure that they are enacted.

Youth justice procedures and practice should also seek to promote the young person's perceptions of the legitimacy of state intervention. Addressing the ambivalence and suspicions of young offenders towards the law and its officials, Matza (1964) claimed that 'the moral bind of law is loosened whenever a sense of injustice prevails'. Thirty years later, Bottoms (1994) has argued that an enhanced sense of legitimacy can increase compliance with legal rules and that 'the way subjects are treated by law enforcement personnel may be of particular importance in enhancing or diminishing a sense of legitimacy'. In a small but significant way, juvenile justice may be able to communicate that the adult world can be fair, tolerant, rational, conciliatory and emotionally literate, without being in any way permissive, lax, sentimental or inconsistent, and thus act as a model for young people to learn from. The youth justice system needs to set a particularly high standard of coherence and fairness, helping to counteract the 'strong sense of a society that really does not like young people very much, especially when they are the offspring of the lower orders' (Taylor 1994).

With these qualities and values in mind, we can visit some important sites within the current juvenile justice system, testing the extent to which they promote legitimacy and reintegration, and illustrating the scope for sound social work practice.

Police detention and questioning

The social worker's initial point of contact with a child in the youth justice system is often in acting as 'appropriate adult' (AA) at the police station. The weight of police power over detained suspects is widely acknowledged, posing a particular challenge in dealing fairly with children who, in one recent study, constituted 17 per cent of detainees (Brown *et al.* 1992). The special status and vulnerability of juveniles held in police detention is clearly recognised by the Police and Criminal Evidence Act 1984 (PACE), although one of the anomalies of the present youth justice system is that PACE safeguards do not apply to 17-year-olds (unless they are mentally disordered). Although parents normally attend as the AA, social workers take this responsibility in around 20 per cent of cases. However, research suggests that they are no more likely than parents to take an active, interventionist role and are frequently either unaware of or unwilling to assert their rights and responsibilities. The PACE Code of Practice makes clear that the AA is not there simply as an observer. The role combines the following tasks: ~

- to advise the young person and to aid her understanding of the process

- to facilitate communication with the young person
- to ensure that interviews are conducted properly and fairly
- to safeguard young persons' rights and to have regard to their welfare.

Littlechild (1996) provides a useful, detailed guide to AA responsibilities, including:

- checking the custody record, obtaining details of arrest and length of detention
- interviewing the young person in private to assess her vulnerability, and requiring this facility at any stage subsequently
- obtaining legal advice where considered necessary
- ensuring that the young person understands the formal caution at the start of interview
- intervening if unfair interview techniques are adopted.

It is worth noting here some findings from research (Evans 1993) about police practice and the interrogative suggestibility of juvenile suspects, which social workers should heed:

- Juveniles were more likely than adults to be arrested where there was insufficient evidence to justify detention. The subsequent interview could thus improperly become a 'fishing expedition'. Some officers perceived the experience of arrest and detention as a potent deterrent to further youthful offending, acting as a warning or 'frightener', and may thus be inclined to pursue this course as a crime prevention measure as well as a crime-solving initiative.

- Juveniles were often not informed clearly what they were accused of, why they were being interviewed or why they had been arrested. Suspects may be left to give an account of what they think they may have done.

- Because juvenile suspects frequently confessed to an offence at an early stage in their interview, in some instances where there was no other evidence against them or the evidence was weak, there is some basis for believing that they confess in the hope of an early release from an uncomfortable or threatening situation, or because they believe that they are likely to be cautioned or warned rather than prosecuted if they co-operate.

- In nearly one in four cases where there was not a ready early confession, the police resorted to 'more persuasive tactics', beyond information-seeking questioning. These included a common device of stating that 'The truth is bound to come out eventually and so there is no point in denying it.' Suspects may be told that owning up is a way of avoiding the police coming round to arrest and interview them again. Evans suggests that such indirect threats can amount to oppressive questioning. Other forms of questioning that may be considered manipulative, unreliable and as exploiting juveniles' interrogative suggestibility include the use of leading questions and 'legal closure' questions (questions that seek to ensure that the suspect provides verbal proof of the necessary legal elements required to establish an offence). These tactics commonly seek to secure the suspect's acceptance of a guilty state of mind or intent, for example that when they trespassed onto property, they intended to steal or that they were acting as 'look out' when others were inside the property (making it burglary). In such instances, the police do most of the talking and the questions asked direct the suspect to particular confirmatory answers. Suspects may agree to statements without understanding their legal implication. The interviewee is not allowed to provide an account in her own words. Interviewers may nevertheless believe that they have secured a full and frank discussion, even though suspects have not necessarily accepted that they have done anything wrong or have accepted that they had done something wrong but without admitting a criminal offence.

- Out of a total of 38 cases in which the police either recorded a full admission or made no clear statement about whether the juvenile had made a full confession, where the researcher assessed that the suspect had denied the offence or made an admission falling short of a full confession, the outcomes were as follows: 12 juveniles were prosecuted; 13 dealt with by caution and 8 given an informal warning. The research did not follow up those prosecuted, although Evans points out that neither the Crown Prosecution Service nor the defence normally listens to interview tapes or seeks to go behind the police judgement, and prosecution case summaries are taken at face value. However, it was of concern that, in nearly 13 per cent of the sample, suspects made clear denials or no clear admissions but were nevertheless cautioned or informally warned. This represented 22 per cent of the total number of cases disposed of in either of these two ways.

Alert and informed AAs can help to ensure that police interviewers adopt a more information-gathering and less manipulative approach, and help to ensure that juvenile suspects understand better the legal implications and possible consequences of what they say. The task is not simply to safeguard the young person's immediate interests, but also to provide the opportunity to begin a supportive relationship, which can lay the foundation for future work, as the following case illustrates.

CASE STUDY

Paul, aged 15, had been arrested for a serious burglary, and a social worker attended as AA because his father, a sole carer, suffered a stress-related illness that was aggravated by the news of Paul's arrest. Paul had already asked for legal representation. Although the case against Paul seemed overwhelming to the AA, it was clear in the first interview that the investigating officers were relying on obtaining Paul's admission rather than presenting clear incriminating evidence. Paul's solicitor thus advised him to make 'no comment'. As Paul's detention extended while the investigating officers pursued further enquiries, the AA initially persuaded the custody officer to allow Paul to sit with him in the custody area, rather than being held alone in a 'detention room' or cell, and subsequently made representations about the unsatisfactory, protracted delay (citing the UN Convention – Article 37(b), see section Children in custody – for good measure!), urging that Paul should be released on bail to return to the police station at a later date. In the interim, the AA had been building a rapport with Paul, gaining a better understanding of his problems, which had been causing him to stay out overnight, sometimes sleeping rough. Paul was eventually released on bail without charge after 10 hours detention, of which only 33 minutes had been spent in interview. The AA obtained a copy of the custody record before leaving the police station (as the failure to expedite a juvenile's detention might subsequently provide the basis for a complaint to the police) and took Paul home, agreeing with him and his father that the youth justice team would remain in contact. The worker considered that there was a strong possibility of a successful prosecution, despite the initial problems in the investigation, and wanted both to support Paul in avoiding further offending in the meantime and to begin helping him in the pre-sentence report (PSR) stage so that the report would be able to demonstrate that Paul was already receptive to supervision, thus enhancing his prospects of a non-custodial sentence. The sentencing court would have to recognise that a Young Offender Institution (YOI) sentence would interrupt work already in progress rather than merely preventing a potential initiative.

Diversion from prosecution

Until 1994 there was broad agreement that 'there should be a presumption in favour of not prosecuting juveniles' among special categories of vulnerable offenders (Home Office Circular 59/1990). Although cautioning had developed on a non-statutory footing, this procedure had acquired the authoritative backing of Home Office National Standards, which have asserted the merits of diversion from unnecessary appearance in criminal courts, dealing 'quickly and simply' with less serious offenders and reducing 'the chances of their re-offending'. This commitment, which has been characterised as 'doing less harm', has nevertheless been weak in a number of respects:

- Although the scope to caution should not preclude an informal warning instead, there is no guidance on the use of this option nor any routine data on its uptake, thus obscuring our understanding of juvenile justice trends.

- Although a caution should not be administered without evidence of guilt sufficient to give a realistic prospect of conviction, an admission of the offence and informed consent, as noted earlier (Evans 1993) the limited available research evidence indicates substantial reliance on ambiguous self-incriminating statements by juveniles or weak evidence, casting doubt on one in five cautioning or informal warning disposals. We know little of the reality of this form of 'bargaining in the shadow of the law'.

- The National Standards offer little guidance on the administration of a caution (or a warning), and police officers are not trained in this procedure. No research has studied the chemistry of the cautioning arena, the engagement and dialogue with the juveniles, despite the belief that this may have a greater direct impact than the theatre of the courtroom. When documentary cameras have occasionally captured the experience, police officers seem to adopt a limited repertoire of techniques, attempting to harangue, belittle or shame the child.

- Over-reliance on 'growing out of crime' and concerns about welfarist net-widening have inhibited the scope to develop resources and strategies to meet children's needs at the cautioning stage, to evaluate their effectiveness and to develop a range of diversionary procedures available for juveniles with persisting involvement in more minor offending.
- The legal effect of a caution in subsequent criminal proceedings against the cautioned person is unclear.

It is thus not surprising that the caution has experienced an eclipse. Despite evidence that, as a general rule, juveniles are prosecuted after they have received two cautions (Evans 1994; Home Office 1994), Home Office Circular 18/1994 actively discouraged the use of more than one caution unless 'the subsequent offence is trivial' or 'where there has been a sufficient lapse of time since the first caution to suggest that it has had some effect'. The Labour Party (1996) subsequently proposed its own version of 'Your first chance is your last chance' by replacing the formal caution with the one-off Final Warning; this will be included in the Crime and Disorder Bill. A Final Warning would 'usually trigger a set of interventions', including assessment of juveniles, working with parents to enhance their supervision, counselling, groupwork, reparation or referral to supervised youth activities. Although this initiative sounds uncompromisingly bullish and inflexible, it has the merit of galvanising attention to children's needs, requiring local authorities to develop imaginative support programmes. The best-known example of 'caution plus' in England is the work of the Northamptonshire Youth Justice Diversion Unit. Two parallel European initiatives impressed the Home Affairs Select Committee (House of Commons 1993) and the Audit Commission (1996):

- *Youth Contract (Denmark).* Suitable young people are referred by the police to the social services agency, which then negotiates a draft contract with the young person and her parents, taking full account of the child's wishes and circumstances. The draft is sent to the police for acceptance or suggested amendment and is then signed and sent to the youth court in readiness for a hearing, not for trial and conviction but for the court to be satisfied that the offence is admitted and the contract accepted.

- *HALT Project (Netherlands).* Aimed at young repeat offenders whose offending is neither entrenched nor of high value, the project receives police referrals of young people who are prepared to participate voluntarily in reparation work (for their victim, if possible), compensation and an educational component addressing the reasons for offending.

In the courtroom

As acknowledged in Chapter 5, courts can seem daunting, distancing and demoralising places for young defendants and their families. Most available empirical evidence of courtroom experience in youth justice relates back to the juvenile court prior to the implementation of the Children Act 1989, which diverted care work to the new family proceedings court, and the Criminal Justice Act 1991, which established the youth court extended in jurisdiction to 17-year-olds, but it is nevertheless worth drawing on those findings for a sense of what prosecution may feel like as a consumer.

The most comprehensive research initiative remains Parker *et al.*'s (1981) initiative to observe 170 sessions of criminal proceedings in two neighbouring juvenile courts and interview a sample of adolescent defendants and their parents. The ethos of the two courts varied markedly. While the legitimacy of both courts was undermined to some extent by perceived pre-court official malpractice, 'City' juvenile court operated in a civil, fair and acceptably rational manner while 'Countryside' court pursued a punitive, repressive, degrading and belittling course that was bitterly resented. Its moral authority was unsurprisingly absent. The overall impression gained from both courts was of largely bemused and powerless consumers who experienced 'routine exclusion and objectification'. The authors recall Emerson's (1968) observation about American juvenile justice:

> The defendant is the subject of a debate between people whose relationship to himself is always vague and whose relation to each other is mysterious.

A quarter of the adolescent sample perceived 'formal courtroom language as part of a conspiracy to exclude, ensnare and befuddle them'. Consumers were predominantly passive or silent, 'a tactical and ultimate line of defence, a final guard against loss of one's self respect and dignity'.

In a subsequent study, Brown (1991) sought to explore the craft of sentencing juveniles, particularly the moral assessment of youthful defendants, by gauging magisterial perceptions, vision and the use of social information in six juvenile courts in northern England from 1985 to 1988. She highlights the absence of true dialogue between sentencer and consumer, and suggests that the 'project' of the juvenile court is to reconstruct individuals as 'information objects, entities amenable to processing'. The court seeks to gather clues and information from professionals about the controllability of youth, according to preconceived perceptions of the pathology of offending, ideal family relationships and the proper use of schooling and leisure time. Brown notes the sensitivity of most defendants to the demands of enrolment and their compliance in learning the rules of the game, the conventions of the occasion and the boundaries of the court's inquiry: 'No desire is shown to understand the meaning of the offence from the child's point of view; rather the child must account for it in the court's terms.'

Apart from efforts to improve dialogue and communication with youth court sentencers, both inside the courtroom and through other liaison channels, social workers can help young people to anticipate their court appearance and to increase their understanding of and participation in proceedings. A simple initiative may be the provision of a guide to proceedings in the local court, taking account of preferred practice and identifying the function of the various participants, the steps in procedure, the scope to be heard and so on. More ambitiously, a pre-trial visit to the courthouse can help to make the experience less alienating. Provision of this service by the Himmat Project, established by West Yorkshire Probation Service and the Calderdale Asian Youth Association in Halifax (Howard League 1994), has proved particularly useful for the local Asian community. Where requested, an Asian project worker is also able to attend the subsequent hearing to offer guidance and information on the day. The Project ('Himmat' literally means 'endurance') also assists in the preparation of pre-sentence reports, helps to explain the sentencing options and participates fully in any supervisory order that is made, thus ensuring that young Asian people both receive this form of sentence more frequently and gain more benefit from the support and assistance provided.

Prior to government, the Labour Party (1996) concluded that the youth court is fundamentally flawed as a means of getting young offenders and their parents to face up to offending. By following the essential characteristics and timetable of adult courts, the youth court process appears irrelevant, confusing and counterproductive:

> The game of the legal process can both inflate the ego of many attention-seeking youngsters and ultimately produce boredom and indifference because it goes on so long. (Labour Party 1996:5)

The Scottish system of Children's Hearings has long provided an intriguing counterweight to the perceived faults of the juvenile court. The Labour Party proposed to borrow and adapt that experience by separating the adversarial task of determining whether an offence has been committed from a more informal and inquisitorial process of disposal, allowing 'wider inquiry into the circumstances and nature of the offending behaviour leading to a plan of action for changing that behaviour'. The court would seek to secure 'the full participation of young offenders and their parents', hearing at first hand their attitude to the offence. Legal representation through legal aid would cease in cases where there is no serious dispute over the facts, allowing direct dialogue with families, who would nevertheless be able to bring 'any friend or representative to help them put their point of view'.

These proposals are now anticipated to be taken forward via a White Paper and the Crime and Disorder Bill, likely to become law in 1998. The introduction of an inquisitorial youth court, placing much greater emphasis on consumer participation, may empower children and parents but will also require greater knowledge, skills and resourcefulness if this opportunity is to be genuinely participative. The Scottish experience suggests that this does not occur readily without considerable facilitative sensitivity on the part of sentencers, and social workers will have far greater potential and cause to help participants to prepare for constructive dialogue.

Legal representation

Ashford and Chard (1997:1) comment that 'advocacy on behalf of young clients is a specialist area undervalued by many criminal defence lawyers':

> As a result of this attitude representation in the youth court is often delegated to the most junior lawyers. In practice, the youth of the client, the frequent chaos of their lives and the complexity of the procedural

rules applicable to children and young person make them an extremely challenging area of defence practice.

Social workers may be well placed to assist children to obtain skilful, experienced legal representation by a solicitor who is able to establish a rapport and communicate effectively with young clients, explaining the law in a jargon-free way and helping them to make informed decisions and give proper instructions. The defence lawyer may also need to deal tactfully with the child's parents, so that they understand what is happening and what is expected of them, while ensuring that instructions are taken from the client rather than from the parent or other adult who may assume to know what is best for the child.

Punishing parents

To encourage parents to strive harder to prevent their children from reoffending, the Criminal Justice Act 1991 converted a previously discretionary power to bind over parents or guardians to exercise proper care and control into a duty to do so, when the child concerned is aged under 16. If the child is subsequently reconvicted, the parent is liable to forfeiture of the sum specified, up to £1,000. There was little evidence at time of implementation that magistrates were anxious to exercise this provision and, in any event, the enforcement procedures are legally obscure. We do not have a clear picture of the uptake of the power since 1992, but a recent small-scale study of youth courts in a Welsh county between July and December 1993 indicates the use of parental bind-overs on 12 (16 per cent) of 77 sentencing occasions (Drakeford 1996). In eight of these instances, it was the child's first conviction, which does not suggest that courts were prompted by a record of parental neglect.

Social work practitioners may thus need to be alert to this possibility and to offer an assessment of family realities that may influence sentencers to opt out of their 'duty' if not satisfied that a bind-over is desirable in the interests of preventing further offending (Criminal Justice Act 1991 s.58(1)(b)). The essential issue to be addressed is whether such a sanction-backed undertaking is likely to improve family relationships and parents' rapport with their children. Parents who can enhance their influence and control are likely to be prompted to try harder on the strength of their child's prosecution, without the need to 'enter a recognisance'. Where a young offender has made a number of court appearances, there may be cause for doubt whether the threat of formal sanctions will prove efficacious in changing patterns of behaviour. If families are experiencing a significant degree of disharmony, lack of cohesion and communication, strain or limited practical or emotional resources, the threat of sanction is likely to be counterproductive, perhaps driving a wedge between exasperated parents and challenging children.

In addition to demonstrating magistrates' confusion about this power, Drakeford interviewed a small sample of parents subject to bind-over. Anxiety about the potential financial forfeit had 'added to the tensions in already combustible households'. Parents felt disempowered and rendered incompetent by their courtroom experience yet simultaneously ordered to act competently, causing a deep sense of unfairness. In addition, the intended psychological impact of binding over seemed to have badly misfired:

> Far from assisting in controlling their children, the bind over had shifted power in the young person's direction: 'she thinks she can do what she likes now and that I'll be the one in trouble. It teaches them to be less responsible, not more.' (Drakeford 1996:254)

Even in instances where the child had been in no further trouble, the bind-over appeared to have made 'no difference whatsoever'. Drakeford concludes that, far from the reinforcement and enhancement of parental authority, 'embitterment and erosion of productive family functioning appear to have been the result'. In the meantime, the bind-over power has been extended to allow courts to require an additional recognisance that parents ensure that the child complies with the requirement of any community sentence imposed (Criminal Justice and Public Order Act 1994). It is worth noting that a bind-over may be revoked on the application of the parent or guardian if the court considers that this would be in the interests of justice, having regard to any change of circumstances since the order was made. While this would be an obvious course if the young person no longer lived with the person bound over, an application could also be appropriate if the bind-over has adversely affected family relationships, and a supportive social work assessment could assist the court's appreciation of such developments.

It is anticipated that the Crime and Disorder Bill will introduce new powers to impose both 'child protection orders' (requiring parents to ensure that their children under 10 do not offend) and 'parental responsibility orders', strengthening requirements and sanctions upon parents in respect of their older children's behaviour. Although intended as part of a more comprehensive package of prevention and intensive support, social workers will need to be alert to the possibility that such measures will exacerbate conflicts between parent and child, and seek to advise courts against the simplistic use of enforcement powers to engineer solutions to fraught family functioning.

Remand opportunities

The legal provisions governing the remand phase of youth justice are complex and the practice arrangements are decidedly patchy, lacking any systematic child care strategy. Concern has mostly focused, quite properly, upon the continuing use of custodial remand of 15- and 16-year-old boys. The phasing-out of juvenile remands to prison service establishments has been government policy since the mid-1970s. Although the 1991 Act contained provisions to end custodial remands for this residual group once sufficient local authority secure accommodation places became available, the transitional provisions remain in force.

The damaging impact of custody upon young people, whether pre-trial or on sentence, will be addressed below and has rightly prompted concern about the lack of pace of provision of alternative local authority secure accommodation, slowly expanding from 257 places in March 1995 to an anticipated 443 places by June 1998. Contrasting the two zones of provision, the Howard League's Commission of Inquiry into penal institutions for the under-18s noted the favourable child-centred ethos of secure units, with broad emphasis upon the quality of relationships, building of trust and dialogue, and explicit recognition of young people's rights and responsibilities. Units nevertheless experienced some degree of negative 'prison culture', exposing residents to bullying and taxing, regional rivalries and tensions between younger and older children. These tensions are set to increase when courts acquire the power to remand 12–14-year-olds to secure accommodation, another innovation of the Criminal Justice and Public Order Act 1994. Secure accommodation can be as disruptive of community ties as is custody, and indeed many boys express a preference for custodial remand if this will afford them better prospects of regular visits. The Commission concluded that secure accommodation should be used as a measure of last resort, the main policy emphasis being upon community provision to enhance the prospects for young defendants in sustaining bail requirements.

The Children Act 1989 Schedule 2, para 7 requires every local authority to take steps designed to reduce the need for children in their area to be placed in secure accommodation.

All remands to local authority accommodation present problems. The placement normally arises out of an unplanned crisis. The child is likely to have little commitment because of the short-term nature of the placement. Older residents influence younger ones in much the same way as in custodial institutions, and this can promote new offending alliances between those sharing residential life. The staff are unlikely to be experienced in working with young people who offend. Group care placements can thus be both expensive, disruptive and inefficient in dealing with young people at a stage when they can easily feel fatalistic or reckless about their predicament and at high risk of further offending.

A comprehensive approach to 'remand management' in youth justice, as advocated by the Social Services Inspectorate (Department of Health 1993), Gibson *et al.* (1994) and NACRO's Juvenile Remand Review Group (1996), includes the following elements for social work priority:

- active intervention to assist bail decision-making at the police station after charge or on first appearance in custody at court, including negotiation with parents or family to facilitate a return home or alternative arrangements with relatives

- providing bail support packages of oversight and activities, to encourage young defendants to comply with bail conditions, to survive the intervening period as constructively as possible, thus enhancing their sentencing prospects

- providing a range of alternative accommodation for young people with no suitable place to stay

- ensuring that 17-year-olds (who remain subject to the same remand provisions as adults) do not 'fall between two stools, being excluded from arrangements for adult defendants but also being regarded as ineligible for facilities for juveniles' (Gibson *et al.* 1994). A NACRO survey of 103 local authorities in 1993 found that 17-year-olds benefited variably from local arrangements as follows: bail information services in 40 authorities, bail support in 51, remand fostering in 20 and supported lodgings or accommodation in 42

- establishing a remand management panel of youth justice workers to consider more difficult-to-resolve individual cases, to promote enhanced remand services and to monitor the use of resources and local remand decisions.

Although such principles are now generally acknowledged, translation into accessible services has been less sure-footed. Among projects that illustrate good practice, identified by the Howard League (1994):

- *Start Point, South Devon.* The project provides eight short-stay beds for young people remanded to local authority accommodation (LAA) or subject to a bail support package, for a maximum of 8 days, offering a breathing space while alternative, more appropriate accommodation is sought. The team prioritises those who would otherwise face a remand in custody. Workers continue to offer support after the resident has moved on and also oversee the needs of other young defendants subject to bail support conditions. Help will commonly include dealing with difficult family relationships, problems of control within the home or substance abuse, as illustrated by this case example.

CASE STUDY

Ben, aged 15, had been staying out at night, becoming involved in theft from motor vehicles. Although the court considered remanding him to local authority care, he was bailed back to his home subject to bail support by project staff. After an initial improvement, he was caught supplying drugs to other pupils at his school and suspended. He was also apprehended in the fraudulent use of his father's cheque book and credit cards. His parents felt they could no longer cope with him. A short period of remand to LAA, staying at the project, allowed successful negotiations with his school and parents so that the court re-bailed Ben back to his home with a more intensive package of bail support, including family counselling, regular individual contact with Ben, work on his drug use and encouragement to pursue new leisure interests.

- *Pre-Trial Intervention Team (PRINT), Cardiff.* Designed to deal with young people facing remand into custody, the PRINT project receives notification from the police of detained young people in time to gather information and make an assessment of the viable options prior to their court appearance. A panel meeting of youth justice workers assesses the risks involved and finalises proposals to put to the court. Support services are designed to reflect the seriousness of the offence, public protection issues and the young person's vulnerable circumstances.

● *Remand Fostering Schemes.* A number of authorities have successfully recruited and trained carers who can offer an intensive, very personal package of care and support that is less intrusive than institutional provision, avoids contact with other young offenders and allows the young person to maintain a higher degree of personal responsibility. The following case example arises from the young offender community project in Southampton.

CASE STUDY

Sandy, aged 17, had spent much of her childhood in care because of severe problems between her and her mother, which left her feeling very isolated and unloved. Shortly after leaving care, Sandy abducted a baby but was discovered soon afterwards with the baby unhurt. After an initial remand to prison custody, where she was housed on the hospital wing to protect her from other prisoners, she was bailed with a condition of residence at a bail hostel some distance away. This was not a satisfactory arrangement, mirroring her previous unhappy experience of residential provision, but allowed space to negotiate her placement with the Smith family. Following bail variation, Sandy remained as a member of the family and made significant progress in learning to talk through her problems. In the light of her improved behaviour and morale, the Crown Court imposed a Probation Order with a requirement that she continued to reside with the Smiths.

● *'Positive Action Contract' (PACT) Schemes.* Run in partnership between the Society of Voluntary Associations (SOVA), the Apex Trust and the Probation Service, PACT schemes aim to help young people aged 17 plus to break a cycle of offending and achieve independence by combining accommodation with a supportive 'provider', assessment of education, training or employment needs and the involvement of a volunteer to befriend and assist participants.

Community supervision

Community practice with young offenders has been heavily influenced by the so-called 'new orthodoxy', developed during the 1980s and placing primary emphasis on viewing juvenile justice as a system. Tactical intervention in that system at key decision-making points aimed to avoid 'net-widening' (or 'mesh-thinning') and to reduce the number of young offenders receiving custodial sentences. Because adherents have believed diversion from deleterious custody to be so intrinsically worthwhile, alternative community programmes have tended to receive more cursory critical attention. Additionally, workers have taken comfort from the belief that adolescent offending is essentially transient and that the main task is to 'hold' delinquent young people successfully in the community and thus weather out this critical phase in their lives (Bottoms 1995).

The comfort provided by these perspectives has been questioned by research on intensive community supervision undertaken by the Cambridge Institute of Criminology. Bottoms and his colleagues (1995) studied a sample of 426 boys (mean age 15.7 years) receiving custody, intermediate treatment and 'straight' Supervision Orders in four local authority areas, yielding full data on 270. Although only recently published, the fieldwork took place over the period 1987–90, but it is nevertheless the best evaluative picture available of contemporary supervision outcomes, which can be summarised conveniently thus:

- Young people and their parents rated intermediate treatment (IT) and staff (especially 'heavy-end IT') very positively. This was particularly striking for the intensive programmes, which entailed substantial restrictions on participants' freedom of movement in leisure time.

- Using a simple 'reconviction or caution' test of re-offending in the 14 months after the end of treatment, there was no evidence that community supervision was better than custody at preventing re-offending. While 81 per cent of the custody subsample re-offended on this test compared with 74 per cent of those receiving heavy-end IT, this was not statistically significant. In terms of 'criminality', as revealed by reconviction patterns and self-reported re-offending, there was some basis for claiming a modest advantage for heavy-end IT over custody, but this was not statistically significant.

- Use of a personal problem checklist to investigate the effect of different interventions showed that the subsample receiving custody perceived themselves as having relatively more personal problems 1 year after the end of intervention, a difference not apparent immediately after intervention. In other words, custody appeared to lead over time to more social problems, which could result indirectly in increased criminality. The Cambridge research did not allow further follow-up, so this hypothesis was not confirmed.

Among proposals for the enhancement of community supervision programmes, Bottoms suggests:

- As well as 'managing the juvenile justice system' by providing 'alternatives to custody', social workers should give more precise attention to the reduction of offending, given the evidence that persistent young offenders are not readily desisting from crime in late adolescence and that their transition to adulthood is often prolonged into their early to mid-20s (as borne out by the Home Office's recent survey of a national sample of young people and their offending: Graham and Bowling 1995).
- Workers should pay more attention to offenders' informal personal social links, to be sustained after intervention, which can act as effective bridges to the community.
- More effort should be made to involve parents in supervision and IT projects. The degree of parental involvement in programmes studied was slight, but nearly half of all parents of children attending heavy-end projects said they would have valued greater involvement.
- Projects should give prominence to 'strong pro-social modelling', that is 'giving offenders, within a framework that they can identify with, a strong lead as to future behaviour', ameliorating attitudes towards school, enhancing problem-solving in conflictual relationships with adults, reducing impulsivity, boosting self-confidence in pro-social activities and so on. In similar vein, the Audit Commission (1996) urged the more imaginative use of 'mentors' or role models to support and encourage young people to change their behaviour patters, as a supplement to formal supervision.

As HM Inspectorate of Probation (1994) note, following a study of the case records for 154 young supervisees in 12 probation areas, 'good practice' proved more difficult than usual to identify with certainty. The Inspectors found 'ample evidence that many supervisees were apathetic and unmotivated, and had disorganised lifestyles or were beset by personal or social problems'. Examples of unimaginative, unenthusiastic, routine practice were seen, but so too were examples of impressive change wrought from unpromising beginnings. Success arose partly from the enthusiasm and empathy of workers prepared to adopt a 'slower, more informal approach', but also depended on the organisation of service delivery to young people. The following case illustration demonstrates some of the qualities that help to promote success without a high level of resources.

CASE STUDY

Rita had left home at 15 and was of no fixed address. She had already had an Attendance Centre Order and was subject to a conditional discharge for theft from members of her family. Now aged 16 and before the youth court again, this time for a number of burglaries, she was remanded to local authority accommodation. In the absence of anything more suitable, she had to be placed in a downmarket bed-and-breakfast hotel. Rita soon expressed a clear preference to move to her boyfriend's bed-sit. The two social workers supporting Rita had concerns about this relationship, the boyfriend being 30 and with a track record of short-term involvement with teenage girls, but respected Rita's choice and wished to build up her fragile self-esteem and competence in decision-making. After consultation with her parents, the workers agreed the move and remained in close contact, providing emotional support, welfare rights advice and a limited degree of financial help, trying to give Rita a better sense of control over her circumstances, while encouraging positive links between Rita and her family.

Faced with an indication from the court that a custodial sentence was being considered, the pre-sentence report successfully proposed a Supervision Order under the Children and Young Persons Act 1969 s.12D, that is as a direct alternative to custody, with a requirement that Rita should undertake specified activities: a 30-day reparation programme, involving her in assisting a local charity. With no small amount of coaxing and encouragement by the social workers, Rita completed this programme, enjoying it sufficiently to continue in contact voluntarily. Although avoiding further property crime, Rita now resorted to street prostitution as an alternative income supplement but was open about this with her social workers, who pursued their earlier course of helping her make informed choices and take responsibility for her decisions, counselling her on the hazards of her behaviour, the potential consequences of prosecution, the likely impact upon her family and the implications for her relationship. Rita was put in touch with a voluntary organisation working with street prostitutes to give her more information and support in both surviving safely for the present and considering her options longer term. Social work advocacy also enabled Rita to be assessed as a housing need priority and to gain tenancy of a council flat, shared with her boyfriend but with the security of being in her name, social services underwriting her rent contribution commitment in view of her age. Her parents provided considerable practical help in establishing her in her new home.

Rita combined street-wise experience with the traits and needs of a much younger child, and the workers used a variety of 'play' techniques to help her express her emotions. Clear questions arose about Rita's upbringing, which had left her so vulnerable and emotionally needy, and the workers were able to gain clues to her past experience, such as her exposure to prolonged bullying at school and a terminated pregnancy at age 13, but felt it was important not to 'impose' counselling upon her before she wished to disclose more of herself, a temptation that could have had counterproductive consequences for Rita's trust in her social workers and her current comparative stability.

The 'near adult'

While bringing 17-year-olds properly within the jurisdiction of the youth court and subject to sentencing powers appropriate for children, the Criminal Justice Act 1991 also introduced flexibility in sentencing 16- and 17-year-olds so that they could be made subject to either 'adult' or 'juvenile' community sentences, thus blurring the boundary of youth justice. Sixteen- and 17-year-olds have acquired the status of 'near adult', a concept devised by the White Paper *Crime, Justice and Protecting the Public* (Cm 965 1990) to reflect this age band's capacity to take greater responsibility for the consequences of their actions. The Act does not specify the basis on which choice of penalty (for example

Supervision Order or Probation Order) should be determined, but the White Paper proposed that disposal should be decided primarily on the basis of the maturity of the offender. Courts would also have regard to local sentencing arrangements and options.

'Maturity' is an elusive and imprecise, stereotype-laden concept and, not surprisingly, the criterion was re-framed in Home Office Circular 30/1992, *Young People and the Youth Court,* as 'the stage of emotional, intellectual, social and physical development in the transition from childhood to adulthood'. The Circular proposed a number of factors that may determine the young person's progress in that transition, such as whether she 'is still in full-time education or in or seeking employment'. The Home Office's subsequent *National Standard for Supervision Orders* (1992) advised that a Probation Order would be more appropriate for 'someone who is already emotionally, intellectually, socially and physically an adult'. It would be a remarkable 17-year-old who could fulfil this description, certainly one highly atypical of those appearing before a youth court. The Association of Chief Officers of Probation (1992) commented that *all* young persons aged under 18 'require assistance in developing skills to live successfully without dependence on others' so should necessarily be dealt with in common by 'juvenile' rather than 'adult' penalties. A small-scale study of 30 under-18s sentenced in 1993 (Stone 1994) clearly indicated that none were leading fulfilled, independent adult lives, 19 remaining dependent on their parents, the others struggling to survive in temporary accommodation or cope with unfamiliar household responsibilities.

Social work and probation practitioners had clearly found it difficult to address sensibly the issue of maturity and the implications for sentencing, and appeared to resort to a number of expedient determinants in advising sentencers. These included: *seriousness of the offence* (in the belief that the sentencer would be more persuaded to adopt a non-custodial sentence if invited to impose an adult community order such as a Combination Order); *age* (a belief that a Probation Order would be more appropriate for an offender approaching her 18th birthday); *previous record* (for example an assumption that a young person who had already served a custodial sentence would be able to cope with adult influences while attending a probation centre as a Probation Order requirement); *quality of supervision* (the assumption that a Probation Order would be supervised with greater vigilance and firmer enforcement. In one instance, the pre-sentence report author considered that, as the young person remained subject to local authority care, a Probation Order would avoid confusion with other roles and responsibilities exercised by social services).

Such dubious attempts to sift young people for sentencing purposes highlight the spurious, contorted and idiosyncratic nature of the hybrid concept of near-adulthood. Far better to maintain a unitary set of supervisory penalties for all young persons under 18, recognising the reality of their difficult transition to independence without falling back on invidious judgements of their qualities, experiences and circumstances. This would prevent the inappropriate placement of children in adult facilities such as probation centres, programmes or hostels. Young people who grow out of crime with the assistance of a Supervision Order would be able to distance themselves more effectively from a clearly youthful phase of their lives, as it appears on their criminal record. The Supervision Order should not be devalued by being incorrectly perceived as a weak or diluted version of statutory supervision, and the onus should rest with local agencies to co-operate in generating a range of resources and programmes suitable for adolescents as part of Supervision Order requirements.

Children in custody

Article 37(b) of the UN Convention states:

> The... detention or imprisonment of the child... shall be used only as a measure of last resort and for the shortest appropriate period of time.

This principle of parsimony was widely accepted in juvenile justice from the mid-1980s and heavily influenced the architects of the 1991 Act. Gibson (1995:67) captures the mood and values of that period thus:

> Custody was seen as the very negation of [constructive community programmes with troublesome young people], a rejection of the offender as irredeemable, unfit to be part of the community, divisive and exclusionary rather than uniting and inclusionary... a recipe for future problems.

High expectations that the use of prison for under-18s would continue to decline have since evaporated. In 1995, 759 15-year-olds, 1,413 16-year-olds and 2,333 17-year-olds were received into custody on sentence. While 17-year-olds have benefited in this respect from their transition into youth justice, 15- and 16-year-olds have clearly experienced a reverse trend. In 1992, 1,252 boys in that age group received custody for indictable offences; in 1994 this had risen to 1,819.

In their study of six juvenile/youth courts before and after the introduction of the 1991 Act, O'Mahony and Haines (1996) found that the proportion of defendants aged 16 and younger given custody had increased from 4.7 per cent to 7.5 per cent, together with an increase in the average length of sentence from just under 4 months in the juvenile court to just over 5 months in the youth court.

Against this upward trend, now buttressed by an increase in the maximum term of YOI detention for under-18s from 12 months to 2 years, the evidence supporting arguments against custody has strengthened. As Bottoms (1995) has noted, community-based practitioners tend to take a particularly pessimistic view of the probable adverse effects of custody, far more so than young people and their parents, and, as pointed out above, should not feel complacently sanguine about the advantageous pay-offs of community supervision. Nevertheless, the custodial environment is particularly hazardous and unsafe for detained children, exposing them to unacceptable risks of bullying, self-harm and neglect, as detailed by the Howard League's Commission of Inquiry into Violence in Penal Institutions for Teenagers under 18 (1995a). Boredom, the shortage of resources, entrenched regional loyalties and rivalries, and the tolerance of a 'natural' pecking order make intimidation and exploitation an invidious and persisting feature of life inside, promoting resort to physical force as a means of problem-solving or conflict resolution. As the Commission noted, 'Taxing and trading within prisons combine with the aggressive and competitive behaviour that often characterises male adolescence.'

Young persons on remand experience particular risks, exposed to poorer physical conditions, a more sterile warehousing regime and placement with older youths. Staff, lacking training in child care responsibilities, may prefer to avoid keeping juveniles separate because 'the younger ones are much calmer with the older ones around'. As Judge Tumim, the Chief Inspector of Prisons, noted in his Annual Report for 1989 (para 6.37, p. 50):

> These youngsters have less in common with young men in their late teens than is generally realised. They are often despised by the older group, resented for their childishness and become victims of intimidation.

In an attempt to convey the reality of life in a typical YOI, the Prison Governors Association resorted to a canine metaphor in its evidence to the Commons Home Affairs Committee: 'a room full of about 50 naughty spaniel pups, with a few Rottweilers, a Pekinese or two and a timber wolf thrown in'.

Of 61 prison suicides in 1994, 11 of the deceased were aged 21 or under. Although less is known of the extent of non-fatal deliberate self-harm in youth custody, 907 such incidents were recorded in young offender establishments (thus excluding young people in local prisons) in 1993–94. The Howard League Commission found that 'most self-harm incidents involving young people are a response to more immediate pressures within the prison system', such as bullying, isolation or the challenge of absurd 'dares'. Judge Tumim commented in his 1990 report on *Suicide and Self-harm in Prison*:

> The young are particularly vulnerable. They are more likely than adults to lack the inner resources to deal with being held in a local prison or remand centre. In prison the most outlandish behaviour can take a grip... Self-mutilation and suicide can become a fixed part of a sub-culture... We strongly believe that prison is no place to hold boys under the age of 17 and that in all cases where removal from the community is necessary, alternative care arrangements should be made.

Such obviously destructive behaviour apart, custodial regimes for young people compare badly with residential care provision in facilities for education, training, recreation, counselling and welfare resources. In the opinion of the Howard League Commission, 'the daily routine for remand prisoners resembles little more than crowd control'. Although school-age teenagers must attend education, the national curriculum does not operate and 'the quality of facilities is often more of a deterrent than an incentive'.

O'Mahony and Haines' study (1996) identified the striking difference between those receiving custodial sentences and the rest of the sentenced youth court population in regard to their offending. On average, they were convicted of almost three times as many offences; over half of them had offended on bail, and they had twice as many previous convictions. Their social need profile is also distinctive. Of 211 15-year-olds dealt with by the Howard League's Troubleshooter Project (detailed below) during 1994, only 18 per cent had been attending education on a regular basis, 14 per cent had a known addiction or were known to be abusing a substance, 22 per cent had been living in the care of a statutory agency and 27 per cent were assessed as 'particularly vulnerable'. The evidence assessed so far indicates our continuing reliance on retributive, degrading, unimaginative regimes that do little or nothing to promote decency and positive values but shape an antisocial outlook and criminogenic survival skills.

Rescue and protection

Although campaigning to secure the end of prison custody for all children, the Howard League's Troubleshooter Project (1995b) has aimed to demonstrate the practical scope for social workers to 'rescue 15 year olds from prison'. Based at Feltham YOI and Remand Centre, the major custodial holding unit for juveniles in the country, the project works with youth justice teams in the community to keep better track of 15-year-olds in the prison system and enhancing their chances. The project tries to enhance the prospects for bail, by mobilising credible bail support packages, and seeks to expedite cases in which bail is refused. Post-sentence, the project initially encourages appeal against sentence. Of 24 cases that went to appeal, eight received a community sentence and nine resulted in reduced custodial sentence. No cases resulted in an increase of sentence. The project has also been able to negotiate temporary release under the provisions of Rule 6 of the YOI Rules, despite a more restrictive approach to this facility. The following case illustrations indicate the potential.

CASE STUDY

Remand stage

Steven was remanded in custody after being charged with attempted burglary with his girlfriend. He had earlier left his home in Ireland because of family difficulties. In a vulnerable frame of mind because he could not see his girlfriend, he attempted to hang himself on his third night in Feltham. Although he was moved to the hospital wing, he made three further serious attempts to throttle himself. The project worker and his social worker made intensive efforts to keep his spirits up and located a place for him in secure accommodation, but the youth court still refused bail, believing that he was best located in the Feltham hospital unit for his own protection. After close liaison with Steven's solicitor, further bail applications were made in the Crown Court and the High Court, eventually securing his remand to secure accommodation where he remained until sentenced to a Supervision Order.

CASE STUDY

Post-sentence

Peter, from a large traveller family, had committed several burglaries, arising from his drug habit, and was sentenced to 11 months YOI. Although he remained drug-free in Feltham, he was fearful of being bullied and was a disciplinary problem. The project worker and his social worker visited him regularly while trying to locate a residential placement that would address his drug problems. No placement was found because of a gap in the range of provision for such young people with drug dependency, but the youth justice team nevertheless proposed a Supervision Order as an alternative to custody (Children and Young Persons Act 1969, s.12D). Although the court did not accept this proposal, his sentence was reduced to 6 months.

CASE STUDY

Temporary release

Richard lived with foster parents prior to his 4 months sentence because of the abuse he had received from his father. He was clearly terrified of custody and had indicated that he would harm himself. The project worker arranged for his foster parents to have special visits to him and to meet his wing governor, helping to pave the way for his temporary release on a well-structured programme supervised by the youth justice team, including curfew from 7.00 pm to 7.00 am. Having served 5 weeks in custody, he spent the final 3 weeks of his sentence following his temporary release package.

In signposting good practice, the project report urges youth justice workers to develop monitoring systems that ensure knowledge of any child entering custody, acquire a better understanding of the needs and circumstances of children in custody through more regular contact, visiting and liaison with prison staff, and exercise proactive advocacy to ensure that a child's period in custody is as short and forward-thinking as is realistically possible. Previous research (see for example McAllister *et al.* 1992) has indicated that many workers feel confused and unenthusiastic in their work with young offenders in custody, missing opportunities to address social work needs.

An initiative at Hull Prison, a Victorian establishment holding 15- and 16-year-old boys on remand, has sought to apply child protection procedures to the custodial environment (Colthup 1996). Although official guidance and regulations interpreting the Children Act 1989 do not mention children in prisons, the duty of a local authority under s.47 of the Act to investigate where there is reasonable cause to suspect that a child is suffering or likely to suffer significant harm applies irrespective of the child's prison status. It has thus proved possible to introduce community child protection procedures in respect of any child held at the prison where abuse or significant harm is suspected. Although immediate removal from the harmful environment is not possible, prison procedures are modified during the process of s.47 enquiries and concerns are expressed to the relevant court encouraging an urgent rethink of the child's remand status. A child needing protection may also be transferred to another custodial establishment. Colthup warns that the provision of child care services in prisons may have the effect of making the incarceration of children appear somehow acceptable, safe and validated, and should be regarded as merely a damage-limitation exercise.

Supervision after release

The statutory requirement of 3 months supervision after release from all YOI sentences is often viewed by social workers as a chore rather than an opportunity by both social workers and young persons, an ineffectually brief and undiscriminating demand upon those who have done their time. The potential importance of this period for those who have been reconsidering their life choices while away from their home base for perhaps the first time is illustrated by the next case illustration.

CASE STUDY

Although 15-year-old Michael's family were shocked by his 90 day YOI sentence for grievous bodily harm and blamed the social worker for this outcome, he survived reasonably well in custody. Supervision after release allowed him to think through his options in fulfilling his wish to leave home at the earliest opportunity to get away from his father's intimidation and emotional instability, and in the meantime to develop coping strategies and assertiveness skills in living tolerably with his father. He was also counselled about his increasing alcohol use. Shortly before supervision expiry, Michael was involved in a violent confrontation with his girlfriend's mother, while intoxicated, and faced a fresh charge of threatening behaviour. His social worker explored the scope for mediation between Michael and the mother, involving an apology and compensation, to which both were agreeable, but the police considered that prosecution was necessary because third parties had also been involved. In advance of the court hearing, the social worker prepared a statement about Michael's difficulties and positive response to supervision, which prompted the youth court to impose a fine rather than adjourn for a pre-sentence report. Although supervision had now expired, the social worker continued involvement, linking Michael to a community music project that welcomed young volunteers with a keen interest in music but also sought to raise their self-esteem and self-awareness.

Conclusion

Youth crime has been described as 'our most complex social problem' (Phillips 1996), a reflection of our anxieties about the impact upon social order of what we now recognise to be the difficult and extended transition to adulthood facing our adolescents. This is not the place to analyse the social and economic policies that have caused profound disillusionment and dissenting lifestyles and moralities for many young people, disenchanted by the erosion of education, work, welfare and housing provision, excluded from traditional spheres of rights and duties, experiencing a major shortfall between aspiration and achievement. Carlen (1996) has explored at length 'the contemporary asymmetries of citizenship' for young people and outlined the need to create a new ethics of inclusion and opportunity. The more modest challenge here is to consider how the formal justice system may do less harm, enhance its prospects of effectiveness and be accorded greater sense of legitimacy.

This chapter has sought to identify both shortfalls and possibilities. Two competing avenues for future emphasis emerge. One pursues the punitive path, further eroding the distinctiveness of youth justice, with greater reliance upon exclusion, whether in custodial institutions, including the new generation of child prisons, the Secure Training Centres, or through community penalties such as the

extension of Curfew Orders with electronic monitoring from age 16-
to 10-year-olds. Such measures attempt to meet the simplistic call to
tidy young people off the streets. Allied measures would seek to
penalise the family further, as illustrated by current proposals to cut
child benefit for parents of children persistently absent from school,
or would encourage exclusionary shaming by abolishing the long-
standing principle that the identities of convicted children should not
be publicised.

The other road seeks to rethink youth justice as an expression of
integrative, educative and restorative values. Building on a raft of
crime preventive measures aimed at preventing the onset of offending
and encouraging desistence from offending, juvenile justice could
attempt to interlink informal with formal sources of social control
more coherently (Graham and Bowling 1995) so that families, schools
and neighbourhoods play an enhanced, influential role.

Walgrave (1996) has suggested that restorative justice could provide
a radically distinct approach to retributive or rehabilitative paradigms
in youth justice, a fully fledged alternative instead of simply an ideas
bank to be raided for techniques that remain a marginal novelty on the
fringe of the familiar dichotomy. Family Group Conferences (FGCs),
pioneered in New Zealand and regarded by Braithwaite and Mugford
(1994) as the best practical expression of reintegrative shaming theory,
combine principles of restoration, mediation, negotiation and victim
empowerment with the strength of family influence. As Graham and
Bowling (1995:102) advocate:

> Based on the principle of putting the needs of the victim and his/her
> family uppermost and restoring the relations between the victim and
> the offender to one of the parity, FGCs place families at the centre of
> the decision making process and thus ensure they take responsibility for
> their young people. This underlying principle is based on the idea that
> the natural development of mutual rights and obligations in families
> provides a foundation for the development of the same in wider social
> relationships, which in turn are seen as a necessary (if not sufficient)
> condition for preventing reoffending.

'Maori justice' may be poised to be the next big idea in the juvenile
justice system, and pilot schemes are already underway, for example in
Basingstoke (*Guardian*, 19 October 1996). The affiliation of such initiatives, whether to the cautioning process or the youth court system itself,
remains to be worked out, as do important conceptual issues such as: the

relationship of restorative justice principles to the seriousness of the offence and the principle of proportionality; securing the co-operation of those concerned, from victim to parent; and the residual place of public protection. Walgrave suggests that the restorative justice model 'will never be the only one in reacting against delinquency but it could eventually become dominant', offering real prospects for a distinctively different, offence-conscious, child-minded and revitalised approach to juvenile justice, a worthy project of legitimacy.

Further reading

Ashford, M. and Chard, A. (1997) *Defending Young People in the Criminal Justice System* (London: Legal Action Group).
Although addressed primarily at lawyers, this book offers a comprehensive and practical guide to law relating to youth justice, from the police station to the end of a custodial sentence.

Graham, J. and Bowling, B. (1995) *Young People and Crime,* Research and Planning Unit Research Study No. 145 (London: Home Office).
An empirical study of offending patterns among young people, emphasising factors that promote desistance from crime.

Haines, K. and Drakeford, M. (1998) *Young People and Youth Justice* (Basingstoke: Macmillan).
This provides a good overview of young people in society, youth and social policy and a recent history of juvenile justice, together with ways of managing youth justice systems and achieving effective work with young offenders within an overarching youth justice philosophy.

Howard League (1994) *The Howard League's Good Practice Guide on Working with Young Offenders* (London: Bellew Publishing).
A handbook illustrating good imaginative practice in youth justice projects in England and Wales at all stages of the criminal justice system.

8

Conclusion

We have argued throughout this book that face-to-face work with children should be an ordinary part of social work and not merely a specialist therapeutic activity reserved for particular children or special cases. This is not only for reasons of fairness and natural justice, but also for effectiveness. In 'outcome-driven' practice, it is important to remember that social work intervention with young people is unlikely to be successful unless someone is able to engage actively with the child and relate to them in a meaningful way (Sinclair *et al.* 1995). It is not productive to give higher priority to decision-making and resource management than to working alongside a child.

Workers who do provide a consistent relationship over time are highly valued by children and young people. As 18-year-old Amy, who has spent the last 14 years with four different sets of carers, recently testified to a group of social work students:

> Sheila my social worker's great. I've known her for five years and she's never missed one single appointment with me – she's been ten minutes late yeah, but she's never let me down.

Amy's statement underlines the symbolic importance of reliability. Sheila has demonstrated that Amy matters as a person and Amy has found in Sheila a secure base who could be relied on. The consistency of Sheila's availability and her refusal to be frightened off by what Amy herself would acknowledge was her truculent and rejecting behaviour has helped this young woman through personal difficulties and placement breakdowns. It has also helped her develop a better sense of self-esteem and self-efficacy.

As we have shown, the diversity of contexts for social work with children leads inevitably to diversity in the nature of the social work practice. Children may be living with foster carers, may be at home with their families or may be cut adrift from their family, fending for themselves. Social workers need to work within that diversity and adapt accordingly, but there are some common factors to be taken into account, relevant both for individual practitioners and for those who plan services, manage and supervise social workers, and provide professional training. As in other areas of social work practice, these can be divided into knowledge, skills and values.

Knowledge

We have demonstrated that the knowledge required to work with children comes from different domains:

- the relevant legal and procedural frameworks
- theories for understanding the child's development and perspective on the world
- ideas for assessing and helping, including different ways of working with children of various ages, backgrounds, cultures and circumstances
- the knowledge workers have about themselves – both their personal strengths and those areas of work with a child that might create a personal resonance that will need to be acknowledged and dealt with.

Skills

There are both practical skills and personal qualities that will make a difference. Social workers need the ability to:

- negotiate with parents, carers and professionals to enable the work to happen
- communicate with children using materials that children themselves find helpful
- remain sensitive to children without being overwhelmed
- sustain a relationship over time in the face of difficulties
- enable children to participate appropriately in decision-making.

Values

Social workers need to think about *why* they are doing this work. As we have suggested, some of this is based on effectiveness. However, we believe that the issue goes deeper than this. In order to argue for this work, often in the face of competing priorities, there is the need for a commitment to the principle that:

- children have the right to be cared for and protected, physically and emotionally
- children have the right to be treated as persons and to have their wishes and feelings listened to and taken into account.

The agency context

Finally, we acknowledge that such professional and personal challenges for child care practitioners working with often very vulnerable children cannot be met fully without the necessary agency framework. This includes the agency not only allowing the time to do the work, but also providing the kind of *skilled supervision* that both places the work with the child in the context of other work with the family and allows the worker time to think, reflect and make sense of what is happening in the work and in the relationship with the child. It is this process which allows the work to maintain its focus and clarifies its direction. The space to think about the child enables the worker to put the emotional content and other potentially stressful aspects of the work in a proper context and is of far more benefit than simply offering what might be more usually described as 'support'.

Since we have argued that work with children should be seen as a regular aspect of the social work role, it follows that supervision for the work should come from the line manager, so it is an area that line managers should also see as part of what they offer team members. Additional consultation on specific aspects of the work and particular techniques may also be needed as practitioners develop greater skill and sophistication. The lack of an outside specialist supervisor should not, however, prevent practitioners from undertaking this work, and workers will need to take responsibility for raising the profile of work with children by making it a regular part of their practice.

From a training perspective, there are a number of issues. Certainly, qualifying training is rarely able to equip new social workers properly with all the knowledge and skills to accomplish this kind of work. It is likely that agencies will need to provide in-service training that gives workers the opportunity to build on some existing skills and knowledge and find ways in which they can become confident and effective when working with children from varied backgrounds and in a range of contexts.

This may seem like a demand for more resources at a time when these are already under pressure, but we know that social workers spend significant amounts of time working to make good decisions for children, to make appropriate plans for children and to sustain children at home and in placements. The whole local authority child care system is built around such processes in order to meet their responsibility to protect the welfare of the child. We believe that the work with children that we have described in this book is not simply desirable as an addition but is inextricably bound up with making that work successful. In so many arenas of their lives, children cannot rely on adults to listen to them. The vulnerable children who come to the attention of social services departments should be able to turn to social workers with the confidence that they will be heard.

Bibliography

Ainsworth, M. D. S., Blehar, M., Waters, E. and Wall, S. (1979) *Patterns of Attachment* (Hillsdale, NJ: Erlbaum).

Aldgate, J. (1988) Work with children experiencing separation and loss, in Aldgate, J. and Simmonds, J. (eds) *Direct Work with Children* (London: Batsford/BAAF).

Aldgate, J. and Simmonds, J. (eds) (1988) *Direct Work with Children* (London: Batsford/BAAF).

Anderson, S., Kinsey, G., Loader, I. and Smith, C. (1994) *Cautionary Tales: Young People, Crime and Policy in Edinburgh* (Aldershot: Avebury).

Archard, D. (1993) *Children: Rights and Childhood* (London: Routledge).

Aries, P. (1973) *Centuries of Childhood* (London: Cape).

Asendorpf, J. B. (1993) Abnormal shyness in children, *Journal of Child Psychology and Psychiatry*, **34**, pp. 1069–83.

Asher, S. R. and Coie, J. D. (eds) (1990) *Peer Rejection in Childhood* (Cambridge: Cambridge University Press).

Ashford, M. and Chard, A. (1997) *Defending Young People in the Criminal Justice System* (London: Legal Action Group).

Association of Chief Officers of Probation (1992) *Seriousness and Proportionality in the Youth Court under the Criminal Justice Act 1991* (London: ACOP).

Attie, I. and Brooks-Gunn, J. (1989) Development of eating problems in adolescent girls: a longitudinal study, *Developmental Psychology*, **25**, pp. 70–9.

Audit Commission (1996) *Misspent Youth: Young People and Crime* (London: Audit Commission).

Bainham, A. (1993) *Children: The Modern Law* (Bristol: Family Law).

Baldwin, S. and Carlisle, J. (1996) *Social Support for Disabled Children and their Families: A Review of the Literature* (London: HMSO/SSI Scotland).

Ball, C. (1995) Youth Justice and the Youth Court: the end of a separate system, *Child and Family Law Quarterly*, 7, pp. 196–208.

Ball, C., McCormack, K. and Stone, N. (1995) *Young Offenders: Law, Policy and Practice* (London: Sweet & Maxwell).

Barclay, P. (1995) Joseph Rowntree Foundation Inquiry into Income and Wealth, vol. 1 (York: Joseph Rowntree Foundation).

Barford, R. and Wattam, C. (1991) Children's participation in decision making, *Practice*, 5(2): 93–102.

Bebbington, A. and Miles, J. (1989) The background of children who enter local authority care, *British Journal of Social Work*, 15: 349–68.

Beccaria, C. (1963) *On Crimes and Punishments* (New York: Bobbs-Merrill).

Bee, H. (1997) *The Developing Child* (New York: HarperCollins).

Bell, V. (1993) Governing childhood: neo-liberalism and the law, *Economy and Society*, 22, pp. 390–405.

Bentovim, A. (1972) Handicapped pre-school children and their families, *British Medical Journal*, 3, pp. 579–81.

Berridge, D. and Cleaver, H. (1987) *Foster Home Breakdown* (Oxford: Basil Blackwell).

Biehal, N., Clayden, J., Stein, M. and Wade, J. (1995) *Moving On: Young People and Leaving Care Schemes* (London: HMSO).

Borba, M. and Borba, C. (1982) *Self-esteem: A Classroom Affair* (San Francisco: Harper & Row).

Bottoms, A. (1994) Avoiding injustice, promoting legitimacy and relationships, in Burnside, J. and Baker, N. (eds) *Relational Justice: Repairing the Breach* (Winchester: Waterside Press).

Bottoms, A. (1995) *Intensive Community Supervision for Young Offenders: Outcomes, Process and Cost* (Cambridge: University of Cambridge Institute of Criminology).

Bowlby, J. (1969) *Attachment and Loss. Vol. 1: Attachment* (London: Hogarth Press).

Bowlby, J. (1979) *The Making and Breaking of Affectional Bonds* (London: Tavistock).

Bowlby, J. (1980) *Attachment and Loss. Vol. 3: Loss, Sadness and Depression* (London: Hogarth Press).

Braithwaite, J. and Mugford, S. (1994) Conditions of successful reintegration ceremonies: dealing with juvenile offenders, *British Journal of Criminology*, 34, pp. 139–71.

Brandon, M. (1996) Attachment in child protection assessments: implications for helping, in Howe, D. (ed.) *Attachment and Loss in Child and Family Social Work* (Avebury: Aldershot).

Brandon, M. and Lewis, A. (1996) Significant harm and children's experiences of domestic violence, *Child and Family Social Work*, 1, pp. 33–42.

Brandon, M., Lewis, A., Thoburn, J. and Way, A. (1996) *Safeguarding Children with the Children Act: Report to the Department of Health* (Norwich: University of East Anglia).

Brannen, J. and O'Brien, M. (eds) (1996) *Children in Families* (London: Falmer Press).

Bridge Child Care Consultancy Service (1995) *Paul: Death through Neglect* (London, published on behalf of Islington Area Child Protection Committee).

British Agencies for Adoption and Fostering (1984) *In Touch With Children – A Training Pack* (London: BAAF).

Brodzinsky, D., Schechter, M. and Henig, R. (1992) *Being Adopted: The Lifelong Search for Self* (New York: Doubleday).

Brown, D., Ellis, T. and Larcome, K. (1992) *Changing the Code: Police Detention under the Revised PACE Codes of Practice*, Home Office Research Study No. 129 (London: HMSO).

Brown, S. (1991) *Magistrates at Work* (Milton Keynes: Open University Press).

Brown, S. (1995) Crime and safety in whose community? Age, everyday life and problems for youth policy, *Youth and Policy*, **48**, pp. 27–48.

Brown, T. and Mitchels, B. (1997) *Loss, Bereavement and Trauma* (Norwich: Watershed Publications).

Bugental, D. B., Mantalya, S. M. and Lewis, J. (1989) Parental attributions as moderators of affective communication to children at risk for physical abuse, in Cicchetti, D. and Carlson, V. (eds) *Child Maltreatment* (New York: Cambridge University Press).

Bullock, R., Little, M. and Milham, S. (1993) *Going Home* (Aldershot: Dartmouth).

Butler, I. and Williamson, H. (1994) *Children Speak: Children, Trauma and Social Work* (London: NSPCC/Longman).

Carlen, P. (1996) *Jigsaw: A Political Criminology of Youth Homelessness* (Buckingham: Open University Press).

Carlile, A. (1996) *Young People and Crime: A Discussion Paper* (London: Liberal Democrat Party).

Children's Rights Development Unit (1994) *UK Agenda for Children* (London: CRDU).

Christensen, E. (1997) Aspects of a preventive approach to support children of alcoholics, *Child Abuse Review*, **6**, pp. 24–34.

Ciccetti, D. and Carlson, V. (eds) (1989) *Child Maltreatment: Theory and Consequences of Child Abuse and Neglect* (New York: Cambridge University Press).

Cippola, J., Benson McGown, D. and Yanulis, M. A. (1992) *Communicating Through Play* (London: BAAF).

Clarke, L. (1996) Demographic change and the family situation of children, in Brannen, J. and O'Brien, M. (eds) *Children in Families* (London: Falmer Press).

Cleaver, H. and Freeman, P. (1995) *Parental Perspectives in Cases of Suspected Abuse* (London: HMSO).

Coleman, C. and Moynihan, J. (1996) *Understanding Crime Data* (Buckingham: Open University Press).

Collins, W. A. (ed.) (1984) *Development during Middle Childhood: The Years from Six to Twelve* (Washington, DC: National Academy Press).

Colthup, N. (1996) Child protection in prison, *Criminal Justice*, **14**, pp. 16–17.

Colton, M., Drury, C. and Williams, M. (1995) *Children in Need* (Avebury: Aldershot).

Corby, B. (1993) *Child Abuse: Towards a Knowledge Base* (Buckingham: Open University Press).

Cretney, S. and Masson, J. (1990) *Principles of Family Law*, 5th edn (London: Sweet & Maxwell).

Crittendon, M. and Ainsworth, M. (1989) Child maltreatment and attachment theory, in Cicchetti, D. and Carlson, V. (eds) *Child Maltreatment: Theory and Research on the Causes of Child Abuse and Neglect* (Cambridge: Cambridge University Press).

Cronin, R. (1997) *Helping Foster Carers to Work with Children who Have Been Bereaved*, dissertation for the Post Graduate Diploma in Advanced Professional Practice with Children and Families Dissertation, University of East Anglia: Norwich.

Cunningham, H. (1995) *Children and Childhood in Western Society Since 1500* (London: Longman).

Dartington Social Research Unit (1995) *Child Protection: Messages from Research* (London: HMSO).

Department of Health (1988) *Protecting Children: Guide to a Comprehensive Assessment* (London: HMSO).

Department of Health (1989) *Care of Children: Principles and Practice in Regulations and Guidance* (London: HMSO).

Department of Health (1991a) *Patterns and Outcomes in Child Placement: Messages from Current Research and their Implications* (London: HMSO).

Department of Health (1991b) *The Children Act 1989 Guidance and Regulations. Vol. 3: Family Placements* (London: HMSO).

Department of Health (1991c) *Working Together* (London: HMSO).

Department of Health (1993) *Young People Detained and Remanded: A Study of Local Authority Remand Services, Social Services Inspectorate Report* (London: Department of Health).

Department of Health (1994) *The Challenge of Partnership: A Guide for Practitioners* (London: HMSO).

Department of Health (1995) *You Are Not Alone* (London: Department of Health).

Department of Health (1996a) *Children Looked after by Local Authorities: Year Ending 31 March 1995* (London: Department of Health).

Department of Health (1996b) *Focus on Teenagers: Research into Practice* (London: HMSO).

Department of Health and Social Security (1985) *Social Work Decisions in Child Care: Recent Research Findings and their Implications* (London: HMSO).

Ditchfield, J. and Catan, L. (1992) *Juveniles Sentenced for Serious Offences: A Comparison of Regimes in Young Offender Institutions and Local Authority Community Homes,* Research and Planning Unit Paper 66 (London: Home Office).

Dodge, K. A., Murphy, R. R. and Buchsbaum, K. (1984) The assessment of intention-cue detection skills in children: Implications for developmental psychopathology, *Child Development,* **55**, pp. 163–73.

Dodge, K. A. and Feldman, E. (1990) Issues in social cognition and sociometric status, in Asher, S. R. and Coie, J. D. (eds) *Peer Rejection in Childhood* (Cambridge: Cambridge University Press).

Dowler, E. and Calvert, C. (1995) *Nutrition and diet in lone parent families in London* (London: Family Policy Studies Centre).

Drakeford, M. (1996) Parents of young people in trouble, *Howard Journal of Criminal Justice,* **35,** pp. 242–55.

Dunn, J. (1988) *The Beginnings of Social Understanding* (Oxford: Blackwell).

Dunn, J. (1993) *Young Children's Close Relationships: Beyond Attachment* (Newbury Park, CA: Sage).

Eekelaar, J. (1986) The emergence of children's rights, *Oxford Journal of Legal Studies,* **6**, pp. 161.

Eekelaar, J. (1991) Parental responsibility: state of nature or nature of the state?, *Journal of Social Welfare and Family Law,* **1**, pp. 37–50.

Emerson, R. (1968) *Judging Delinquents* (Chicago: Aldine).

Epstein, C. and Keep, G. (1995) What children tell ChildLine about domestic violence, in Saunders, A. *It Hurts Me Too: Children's Experiences of Domestic Violence and Refuge Life* (WAFE/NISW/ChildLine).

Erikson, E. (1968) *Identity; Youth and Crisis* (New York: Norton).

Evans, R. (1993) *The Conduct of Police Interviews with Juveniles,* Royal Commission on Criminal Justice Research Study No. 8 (London: HMSO).

Evans, R. (1994) Cautioning: counting the cost of retrenchment, *Criminal Law Review,* pp. 566–75.

Evans, R. and Ferguson, T. (1991) *Comparing Different Juvenile Cautioning Systems in One Police Force Area,* Report to the Home Office Research and Planning Unit (London: Home Office).

Fahlberg, V. (1988) *Fitting the Pieces Together* (London: BAAF).

Fahlberg, V. (1994) *A Child's Journey Through Placement* (London: BAAF).

Family Rights Group (1995) *Partnership Training Pack* (London: FRG).

Farmer, E. and Owen, M. (1995) *Child Protection Practice: Private Risks and Public Remedies* (London: HMSO).

Ferguson, E. (1996) Full of woe or far to go? The nation's children on trial, *Observer,* 9 June.

Fletcher, B. (1993) *Not Just a Name* (London: National Consumer Council).

Franklin, B. (1995) The case for children's rights: a progress report, in Franklin, B. (ed.) *The Handbook of Children's Rights* (London: Routledge).

Fratter, J., Rowe, J., Sapsford, D. and Thoburn, J. (1991) *Permanent Family Placement: A Decade of Experience* (London: BAAF).

Freeman, M. (1983) *The Rights and Wrongs of Children* (London: Frances Pinter).

Freeman, M. (1992) *Children, their Families and the Law: Working with the Children Act* (Basingstoke: Macmillan).

Frost, N. and Stein, M. (1989) *The Politics of Child Welfare* (London: Harvester Wheatsheaf).

Garbarino, J., Stott, F. M. and Faculty of the Erikson Institute (1992) *What Children Can Tell Us? Eliciting, Interpreting and Evaluating Critical Information from Children* (San Francisco: Jossey-Bass).

Garfinkel, H. (1956) Conditions of successful degradation ceremonies, *American Journal of Sociology,* **61**, pp. 420–4.

Gibbons, J., Conroy, S. and Bell, C. (1995) *Operating the Child Protection System: A Study of Child Protection Registers* (London: HMSO).

Gibson, B. (1995) Young people, bad news and enduring principles, *Youth and Policy,* (48), pp. 64–70.

Gibson, B., Cavadino, P., Rutherland, A., Ashworth, A. and Harding, J. (1994) *The Youth Court One Year Onwards* (Winchester: Waterside Press).

Gilligan, C. (1982) *In a Different Voice* (London: Harvard Press).

Gordon, L. (1989) *Heroes of their own Lives: the Politics and History of Family Violence* (London: Virago).

Graham, J. and Bowling, B. (1995) *Young People and Crime,* Research and Planning Unit Research Study No. 145 (London: Home Office).

Gulbenkian Foundation Commission (1995) *Children and Violence: Report of the Commission on Children and Violence* (London: Gulbenkian Foundation).

Hagell, A. and Newburn, T. (1994) *Persistent Young Offenders* (London: Policy Studies Institute).

Hammarberg, T. (1995) Preface, in Franklin, B. (ed.) *The Handbook of Children's Rights* (London: Routledge).

Hardiker, P., Exton, K. and Barker, M. (1991) *Policies and Practices in Preventive Child Care* (Aldershot: Gower).

Harding, L. Fox (1991) *Perspectives in Child Care Policy* (Harlow: Longman).

Hardyment, C. (1983) *Dream Babies* (London: Jonathan Cape).

Harris, P. (1989) *Children and Emotion: The Development of Psychological Understanding* (Oxford: Blackwell).

Harrison, C. and Masson, J. (1994) Working in partnership with lost parents: issues of theory and practice, *Adoption and Fostering*, **18**, pp. 40–4.

Haviland, J. M. and Lelwica, M. (1987) The induced affect response: 10-week-old infants' responses to three emotional expressions, *Developmental Psychology*, **23**, pp. 97–104.

Hearn, B. (1995) *Child and Family Support and Protection: A Practical Approach* (London: National Children's Bureau).

Hendrick, H. (1990) Constructions and reconstructions of British childhood: an interpretive survey, 1800 to the present, in James, A. and Prout, A. (eds) *Constructing and Reconstructing Childhood* (Brighton: Falmer).

Herbert, M. (1987) *Conduct Disorders of Childhood and Adolescence* (Chichester: John Wiley).

Herbert, M. (1999) Adolescence, in Davies, M. (ed.) *The Blackwell Companion to Social Work* (Oxford: Blackwell).

Hill, M., Laybourn, A. and Brown J. (1996) Children of parents who misuse alcohol: a study of services and needs, *Child and Family Social Work*, **1**, pp. 159–67.

HM Inspectorate of Probation (1994) *Young Offenders and the Probation Service: Report of a Thematic Inspection* (London: Home Office).

HMSO (1988) Report of Inquiry into Child Abuse in Cleveland, Cm 412, (London: HMSO).

Hoggett, B. (1993) *Parents and Children: The Law of Parental Responsibility*, 4th edn (London: Sweet & Maxwell).

Home Office (1927) *Report of the Committee on the Treatment of Young Offenders*, Cmnd 2831 (London: HMSO).

Home Office (1992) *Young People and the Youth Court*, Home Office Circular 30/1992, (London: Home Office).

Home Office (1992) National Standards for Supervision of Offenders in the Community (London: Home Office).

Home Office (1994) *The Cautioning of Offenders*, Home Office Circular 18/1994, (London: Home Office).

Houghton-James, H. (1994) Children divorcing their parents, *Journal of Social Welfare and Family Law*, **16**, pp. 185–99.

House of Commons (1993) *Juvenile Offenders. Sixth Report of the Home Affairs Select Committee* (London: HMSO).

Howard League (1994) *The Howard League's Good Practice Guide on Working with Young Offenders* (London: Bellew Publishing).

Howard League (1995a) *Banged Up, Beaten Up, Cutting Up: Report of Commission of Inquiry into Violence in Penal Institutions for Teenagers under 18* (London: Howard League).

Howard League (1995b) *Troubleshooter: A Project to Rescue 15 Year Olds from Prison* (London: Howard League).

Howe, D. (1995) *Attachment Theory for Social Work Practice* (Basingstoke: Macmillan).

Howe, D. and Hinings, D. (1995) Reason and emotion in social work practice: managing relationships with difficult clients, *Journal of Social Work Practice*, **9**, pp. 5–14.

Hunter, F. T. and Youniss, J. (1982) Changes in functions of three relations during adolescence, *Developmental Psychology*, **18**, pp. 806–11.

James, A. and Prout, A. (eds) (1990) *Constructing and Reconstructing Childhood* (London: Falmer Press).

James, A. and Prout, A. (1996) Strategies and structures: towards a new perspective on children's experiences of family life, in Brannen, J. and O'Brien, M. (eds) *Children in Families: Research and Policy* (London: Falmer Press).

James, G. (1994) *Study of Working Together 'Part 8' Reports: Discussion Report for ACPC Conference 1994* (London: Department of Health).

Jenks, C. (1996) The postmodern child, in Brannen, J. and O'Brien, M. (eds) *Children in Families* (London: Falmer Press).

Jewett, C. (1994) *Helping Children Cope with Separation and Loss*, 2nd edn (London: Batsford/BAAF).

Johnson, T. and Parker, V. (1996) *Is a Persistent Young Offender a 'Child in Need'?* (London: Rainer Foundation).

Jones, A. and Butt, J. (1995) *Taking the Initiative* (London: NSPCC/Race Equality Unit).

Joseph Rowntree Foundation (1995) *Income and Wealth: Report of the JRF Inquiry Group* (York: Joseph Rowntree Foundation).

'Justice' (1996) *Children and Homicide: Appropriate Procedures for Juveniles in Murder and Manslaughter Cases* (London: Justice).

Kaganas, F., King, M. and Piper, C. (1995) *Legislating for Harmony: Partnership under the Children Act 1989* (London: Jessica Kingsley Publishers).

Kelly, L. (1992) The connections between disability and child abuse: a review of the research evidence, *Child Abuse Review*, **1**, pp. 157–67.

Kidscape (1994) *Bullying Pays! A Survey of Young Offenders* (London: Kidscape).

King, M. and Piper, C. (1995) *How the Law Thinks About Children*, 2nd edn (Aldershot: Arena).

Klaus, H. M. and Kennell, J. H. (1976) *Maternal Infant Bonding* (St Louis: Mosby).

Krisberg, B. and Austin, J. (1993) *Reinventing Juvenile Justice* (Newbury Park, CA: Sage Publications).

Kroll, B. (1995) Working with children, in Kagansas, F., King, M. and Piper, C. (eds) *Legislating for Harmony: Partnership under the Children Act 1989* (London: Jessica Kingsley Publishers).

Kumar, V. (1993) *Poverty and Inequality in the UK: the Effects on Children* (London: National Children's Bureau).

Labour Party (1996) *Tackling Youth Crime: Reforming Youth Justice* (London: Labour Party).

Liebling, A. (1992) *Suicides in Prison* (London: Routledge).

Littlechild, B. (1996) *The Police and Criminal Evidence Act 1984: The Role of the Appropriate Adult* (Birmingham: BASW).

Loader, I. (1996) *Youth, Policing and Democracy* (Basingstoke: Macmillan).

Longford, Lord (1964) *Crime: A Challenge to Us All*, Report of a Labour Party Study Group (London: Labour Party).

Lord Chancellor's Department (1995) *The Children Act Advisory Committee Annual Report 1994/1995* (London: Lord Chancellor's Department).

Lynes, D. and Goddard, J. (1995) *The View from the Front: The User View of Child Care in Norfolk* (Norwich: Norfolk County Council Social Services).

Lyon, C. and Parton, N. (1995) Children's rights and the Children Act 1989, in Franklin, B. (ed.) *The Handbook of Children's Rights* (London: Routledge).

McAllister, D., Bottomley, K. and Liebling, A. (1992) *From Custody to Community: Throughcare for Young Offenders* (Aldershot: Avebury).

Macdonald, S. (1991) *All Equal under the Act?* (London: Race Equality Unit).

McElrea, F. (1994) Justice in the community: the New Zealand experience, in Burnside, J. and Baker, N. (eds) *Relational Justice: Repairing the Breach* (Winchester: Waterside Press).

Matza, D. (1964) *Delinquency and Drift* (New York: John Wiley).

Maxime, J. (1986) Some psychological aspects of black self-concept, in Ahmed, S., Cheetham, J. and Small, J. (eds) *Social Work with Black Children and Their Families* (London: Batsford/BAAF).

Morris, S. and Wheatley, H. (1994) *Time to Listen: the Experiences of Children in Foster and Residential Care: A ChildLine Study* (London: ChildLine).

Mulhearn, G. (1996) Network conferencing with young people, in Morris, K. and Tunnard, J. (eds) *Family Group Conferences: Messages from UK Practice and Research* (London: Family Rights Group).

NACRO (1996) *Safe and Secure: Ending Remands to Prison for 15 and 16 Year Old Boys* (London: NACRO).

National Commission of Inquiry into the Prevention of Child Abuse (1996) *Childhood Matters* (London: HMSO).

NCH (1994) Messages from children: children's evaluation of the professional response to child sexual abuse. Interim report.

NCH Action for Children (1996) *Still in Need: Refocusing Child Protection in the Context of Children in Need* (London: NCH).

Newell, P. (1991) *The UN Convention and Children's Rights in the UK* (London: National Children's Bureau).

Nielsen, L. (1987) *Adolescent Psychology: A Contemporary View* (London: Holt, Rinehart & Winston).

Oaklander, V. (1978) *Windows to our Children* (New York: Real People Press).

O'Donnell, I. and Edgar, K. (1996) *Victimisation in Prisons,* Research Findings No. 37 (London: Home Office Research and Statistics Directorate).

O'Mahoney, D. and Haines, K. (1996) *An Evaluation of the Introduction and Operation of the Youth Court,* Research and Planning Unit Research Study No. 152 (London: Home Office).

Packman, J. (1993) From prevention to partnership: child welfare services across three decades, in Pugh, G. (ed.) *30 Years of Change for Children* (Derby: NCB).

Parker, H., Casburn, M. and Turnbull, D. (1981) *Receiving Juvenile Justice* (Oxford: Basil Blackwell).

Parker, H., Summer, M. and Jarvis, G. (1989) *Unmasking the Magistrates* (Milton Keynes: Open University Press).

Parker, R., Ward, H., Jackson, S., Aldgate, J. and Wedge, P. (1991) *Looking After Children: Assessing Outcomes in Child Care* (London: HMSO).

Parton, N. (1991) *Governing the Family: Child Care, Child Protection and the State* (Basingstoke: Macmillan).

Parton, N. (ed.) (1996) *Social Theory, Social Change and Social Work* (London: Routledge).

Pearson, G. (1983) *Hooligan: A History of Respectable Fears* (London: Macmillan).

Phillips, M. (1996) *Observer,* 24 November.

Phillips, M. (1995) Issues of ethnicity and culture, in Wilson, K. and James, A. (eds) *The Child Protection Handbook* (London: Baillière Tindall).

Pizzey, S. and Davis, J. (1995) *A Guide for Guardians ad Litem in Public Law Proceedings under the Children Act 1989* (London: HMSO).

Prior, V., Lynch, M. and Glaser, D. (1995) *Messages from Children: Children's Evaluations of the Professional Response to Child Sexual Abuse* (interim report) (London: NCH Action for Children).

Pugh, G. and Rouse-Selleck, D. (1995) Listening to and communicating with young children, in Davie, R., Upton, G. and Varma, V. (eds) *The Voice of the Child: A Handbook for Professionals* (London: Falmer Press).

Reder, P. and Duncan, S. (1995) The meaning of the child, in Reder, P. and Lucey, C. (eds) *Assessment of Parenting: Psychiatric and Psychological Contributions* (London: Routledge).

Reder P., Duncan, S. and Gray, M. (1993) *Beyond Blame: Child Abuse Tragedies Revisted* (London: Routledge).

Richman, N., Stevenson, J. and Graham, P. (1982) *Pre-School to School: A Behavioural Study* (London: Academic Press).

Rowe, J., Cain, H., Hundleby, M. and Keane, A. (1984) *Long Term Foster Care* (London: Batsford/BAAF).

Rowe, J. and Lambert, L. (1973) *Children who Wait* (London: ABAA).

Russell, P. (1996) Children with disabilities and special needs: current issues and concerns for child protection procedures, in Platt, D. and Shemmings, D. (eds) *Making Enquiries into Alleged Child Abuse: Partnership with Families* (Brighton: Pavilion Publishing).

Rutherford, A. (1996) Tackling youth crime: reforming youth justice, *Criminal Justice*, **14**, p. 3.

Rutter, M. and Rutter, M. (1993) *Developing Minds: Challenge and Continuity across the Life Span* (Harmondsworth: Penguin).

Rutter, M., Quinton, D. and Hill, J. (eds) (1990) Adult outcomes of institution-reared children: males and females compared, in Robins, L. N. and Rutter, M. *Straight and Devious Pathways from Childhood to Adulthood* (Cambridge: Cambridge University Press).

Ryan, V. and Wilson, K. (1996) *Case Studies in Non-directive Play Therapy* (London: Baillière Tindall).

Schofield, G. (1994) *The Youngest Mothers* (Aldershot: Avebury).

Schofield, G. (1996) Protection and loss: the impact of separation on the abused and neglected child, in Lindsay, B. and Elsegood, J. (eds) *Working with Children in Grief and Loss* (London: Baillière Tindall).

Schofield, G. and Thoburn, J. (1996) *Child Protection: The Voice of the Child in Decision Making* (London: Institute of Public Policy Research).

Scutt, N. (1995) Child advocacy: getting the child's voice heard, in Cloke, C. and Davies, M. (eds) *Participation and Empowerment in Child Protection* (London: Pitman).

Scutt, N. and Stephens, J. (1995) *Social services- NSPCC-Yes- Child Advocacy Project* (Plymouth: Devon Social Services Department).

Seligman, M. E. P. (1975) *Helplessness: On Depression and Death* (San Francisco: Freeman).

Selwyn, J. (1996) Ascertaining children's wishes and feelings in relation to adoption, *Adoption and Fostering*, **20**, pp. 14–20.

Shemmings, D. (1996) *Children's Involvement in Child Protection Conferences*, Social Work Monograph (Norwich: University of East Anglia).

Shepherd, A. M. (1994) *Ensuring Children's Voices Are Heard in the Child Protection Process and Child Care Decision Making: Strategies for Improving Policy and Practice*, dissertation from the Advanced Certificate, University of East Anglia.

Sheridan, M. (1973) *From Birth to Five Years* (Windsor: NFER-Nelson).

Sinclair, R (1993) High/Scope: Does it enhance children's life chances? Introducing the High/Scope Curriculum into Ireland, in Ferguson, G., Gilligan, R. and Torode, R. (eds) *Surviving Childhood Adversity: Issues for Policy and Practice* (Dublin: Social Studies Press).

Sinclair, R., Garnett, L. and Berridge, D. (1995) *Social Work and Assessment with Adolescents* (London: NCB).

Sluckin, W., Herbert, M. and Sluckin, A. (1983) *Maternal Bonding* (Oxford: Blackwell).

Smith, S. (1994) *Learning from Disruption* (London: BAAF).

Solberg, A. (1990) Negotiating childhood: changing constructions of age for Norwegian children, in James, A. and Prout, A. (eds) *Constructing and Reconstructing Childhood* (London: Falmer Press).

Stainton Rogers, R. and W. (1992) *Stories of Childhood: Shifting Agendas of Child Concern* (London: Harvester Wheatsheaf).

Stein, M. and Carey, K. (1986) *Leaving Care* (Oxford: Blackwell).

Stein, M., Rees, G. and Frost, M. (1994) *Running the Risk: Young People on the Streets of Britain Today* (London: Children's Society).

Stewart, J., Smith, D. and Stewart, G. (1994) *Understanding Offending Behaviour* (Harlow: Longman).

Stone, N. (1994) Sentencing the near adult, *Justice of the Peace*, **158**, pp. 595–7.

Stone, W. (1991) *Sukina: an Evaluation Report of the Circumstances Leading to Her Death* (London: Bridge Child Care Consultancy Service).

Streissguth, A. P., Aase, J. M., Clarren, S. K., Randels, S. P., LaDue, R. A. and Smith, D. F. (1991) Fetal alcohol syndrome in adolescents and adults, *Journal of the American Medical Association*, **265**, pp. 1961–7.

Sugarman, L. (1986) *Life-span Development: Concepts, Theories and Interventions* (London: Methuen).

Sykes, G. and Matza, D. (1957) Techniques of neutralisation: a theory of delinquency, *American Sociological Review*, **22**, pp. 664–70.

Taylor, I. (1994) Foreword to Anderson, S., Kinsey, R., Loader, I. and Smith, C. *Cautionary Tales: Young People, Crime and Policing in Edinburgh* (Aldershot: Avebury).

Thoburn, J. (1990) *Success and Failure in Permanent Family Placement* (Aldershot: Avebury).

Thoburn, J. (1994) *Child Placement: Principles and Practice*, 2nd edn (Aldershot: Arena).

Thoburn, J. (1996) Psychological parenting on child placement: 'but we want to have our cake and eat it', in Howe, D. (ed.) *Attachment and Loss in Child and Family Social Work* (Avebury: Aldershot).

Thoburn, J., Lewis, A. and Shemmings, D. (1995) *Paternalism or Partnership? Family Involvement in the Child Protection Process* (London: HMSO).

Thoburn, J., Brandon, M., Lewis A. and Way, A. (1996) *Safeguarding Children with the Children Act 1989: A Report to the Department of Health* (Norwich: University of East Anglia).

Truax, C. B. and Carkhuff, R. B. (1967) *Towards Effective Counselling and Psychotherapy* (Chicago: Aldine).

Trowell, J. (1996) Understanding the child: the importance of thinking about the child's feelings, in Batty, D. and Cullen, D. (eds) *Child Protection: The Therapeutic Option* (London: BAAF).

Tumim, S. (1990) *Report of a Review by HM Chief Inspector of Prisons for England and Wales of Suicide and Self-Harm in Prison Service Establishments*, Cm 1383 (London: HMSO).

Tunstill, J., Aldgate, J., Wilson, M. and Sutton, P. (1996) Crossing the organisational divide: family support services, *Health and Social Care in the Community*, 4, pp. 41–9.

Walgrave, L. (1996) Restorative juvenile justice, in Asquith, S. (ed.) *Children and Young People in Conflict with the Law*, Research Highlights in Social Work No. 30 (London: Jessica Kingsley Publishers).

Warner, M. (1994) *Managing Monsters* (London: Vintage).

Wheen, F. (1996) Swish of the big stick, *Guardian*, 31 October.

White, R., Carr, P. and Lowe, N. (1995) *The Children Act in Practice*, 2nd edn (London: Butterworth).

Williams, J. E. and Best, D. L. (1990) *Measuring Sex Stereotypes: A Multination Study* (Newbury Park, CA: Sage).

Wilson, K., Kendrick, P. and Ryan, V. (1992) *Play Therapy: A Non-directive Approach for Children and Adolescents* (London: Baillière Tindall).

Winnicott, C. (1964) *Child Care and Social Work* (Hitchin: Codicote Press).

Winnicott, C. (1989) Communicating with children, in Morgan, S. and Righton, P. (eds) *Child Care: Concerns and Conflicts* (Hodder & Stoughton: London).

Winnicott, D. W. (1965) *The Maturational Processes and the Facilitative Environment* (New York: International Universities Press).

Author Index

Subject Index